Making Friends with Cancer

By Dawn Nelson

FINDHORN
Press

First published by Findhorn Press in 2000

ISBN 1-899171-38-X

British Library Cataloguing-in-Publication Data.
A catalogue record for this book is available from the British Library.

Library of Congress Catalog Card Number: 00-105100

Layout by Pam Bochel

Front cover design by Dale Vermeer

Printed and bound in the USA

Published by
Findhorn Press

The Park, Findhorn
Forres IV36 3TY
Scotland
Tel 01309 690582
Fax 01309 690036

P.O. Box 13939
Tallahassee
Florida 32317-3939, USA
Tel 850 893 2920
Fax 850 893 3442

e-mail info@findhornpress.com
findhornpress.com

Contents

for my family,

for myself,

and for

all those who yearn for healing

Acknowledgments

*Sometimes our light goes out but is blown
into flame by another human being.
Each of us owes our deepest thanks to those
who have rekindled this light.*

Sharon Bruckman

The support for healing which I received from family, friends, students, teachers, colleagues, and health care professionals during my cancer diagnosis and treatment rekindled the flame of health in me and thus helped bring this book into being. To each of these individuals and to others whose names are not known to me, I am deeply grateful. Some gave and continue to give daily support and love which sustains, nourishes, and enriches my life. Others came forward to share their time, energy, and unique skills during this challenging period.

I thank my husband, Barry Barankin, an extraordinary human being; my three remarkable and beautiful children—Brianna, Michael, and Meghan; my future daughter-in-law, Sally Regan; my mother and father in-law, Claire and Bob; Philadelphia cousins, Linda and Steve; and my relatives in southern California, Kansas, and Arizona.

I thank our extended family and closest friends: Doug, Katherine and Stephan, Dick and Joanne, and Lawrence; our long-time friends—Jeff and Dutch, Jerie, Kathryn, and Jay. I thank Willow, the embodiment of compassionate care. I thank fellow parents: Becky, Lauren, Pat, Sue and Charlie, LaWanda and Carrie Zagota; my "Moms over Forty" group: especially Cecily, Diane, Linda, Margarite, and Terry; and Cecily's daughter, Carrie, for her piano composition, "Dawn is Winning Now."

I thank my colleagues, friends, and students in the Enlightenment Intensive community, the Buddhist monks, the congregation in Wichita, Anne Marie and the other Sisters of St. Joseph in Boston, our friends in Japan, and the friends of friends who put their attention on me or added their thoughts and prayers to the healing circle organized on my behalf.

I thank the members of Shir Neshama Chavurah Alef—an exceptional group of men and women whose combined acts of kindness fed me, and continue to feed me and my family, in myriad ways—Audrey, Bruce, Debbie, Steve, Edward, Suzanne, Jan, Michael, Janet, Paul, Janice, Joel, Joi, Sherrie, Craig, Sonya, and Rabbi Groesberg, as well as the children of the Chavurah, symbols of hope and future strength.

I thank my husband's colleagues, as well as staff members and students at the Head Royce School, especially Cathy, Crystal, Anne, Carl, David (and Debbie), Kit, Jan, Jane (and Jon), Amy, Heather, and the senior class of 1998.

I thank Daniel, Sue, Barbara, Stephan, Jane, and Chris for their gifts of professional services and for their gentle touch. I thank the COMPASSIONATE TOUCH® training sponsors and students who waited patiently until postponed workshops could be rescheduled.

I thank Ann Lurie, Kathleen, Gary and Owen, Flora, Shirley, Valerie, Debby, Trish, and others who sent unique healing gifts through the mail, the many friends and acquaintances who sent greeting cards and letters, and Lisa who mailed me a different beautiful card every single week for over six months.

I thank my wise healers, inside and outside of the medical profession: Dr. Isaac Cohen, Nancy Fitzgerald, Dr. John Simmons, and

Dr. John Tatman. I thank Robin as well as Bella, Norma, and the other angels of mercy in the oncology infusion units; I thank Jesse and Helen, the needle stick saints in the lab.

I thank Karl Mondon for his material and spiritual generosity. I thank Karl and James Dawson for their photographic contributions to this book.

In addition I thank Pam Bochel, and I express my heartfelt gratitude to Thierry Bogliolo and his wife, Karin, for their graciousness, for their integrity, and for bringing the book into material reality.

Foreword

A dialogue with Dr Bernie Siegel

Bernie Siegel: Dawn, while I admire all you have done, I must agree with someone at one of your workshops that the title of your book, *Making Friends with Cancer*, may not be the best way of expressing its contents. Cancer as a teacher, gift, blessing, etc. because of what it led to, would be more to the point it seems to me.

Dawn Nelson: The title arose in my consciousness when I was coping with my cancer diagnosis, long before I thought of writing the book. It seemed to stem from an old childhood adage I remembered which, in my mind, was connected to friendship: "He drew a circle that shut me out — heretic, rebel, a thing to flout. But love and I had the wit to win. We made a circle that drew him in." That is what I decided to do with my cancer.

Bernie Siegel: I'd say your circle story could have become the title in some way. Making cancer a part of your life and taking it in I can see and even calling it a blessing but friends is a strange concept. We treat friends in a way I don't think I would treat cancer if I had it.

Dawn Nelson: I've used the word friend not in the usual definitive meaning of mutual respect, attachment, trust, etc. but in a secondary meaning of "not actually a foe" or of friendly being "not hostile" and perhaps even a possible opening to the concept of cancer becoming that which "aids or promotes" in its eventual outcome. At the end of my talk at the conference in Germany when a woman in the audience had difficulty with the words I was using in relation to cancer, another woman waited patiently in line to speak to me after my talk and, with tears streaming down her face, thanked me, saying she completely understood what I was saying and that my attitude was the exact same one she and her husband were adopting in relation to his cancer. I imagine most people will fall somewhere in between those two responses to the unusual use of the terminology.

Bernie Siegel: What you say is important and meaningful and I hope we can get this dialogue into your book.

Life is so generous a giver, but we, judging its gifts by their covering, cast them away as ugly or heavy, or hard. Remove the covering, and you will find beneath it a living splendor, woven of love, by wisdom with power.

Welcome it, grasp it, and you touch the angel's hand that brings it to you. Everything we call a trial, a sorrow or a duty, believe me, that angel's hand is there; the gift is there,
and the wonder of an overshadowing presence. Our joys too: be not content with them as joys. They too conceal divine gifts.

And so, at this time, I greet you.
Not quite as the world sends greetings, but with profound esteem and with the prayer that for you, now and forever, the day breaks, and the shadows flee.

Fra Giovanni, A.D. 1513

Introduction

When we are no longer able to change a situation,
we are challenged to change ourselves.

Victor Frankl

A decade ago thousands of people, including a number of my friends and acquaintances, lost their homes and all their belongings to a devastating fire-storm that blew out of control in the Berkeley-Oakland hills. In the chaos that followed, some people's anger raged hotter than the fire. Some people's mourning lasted years. Some have never fully recovered from the trauma. A few people, after the initial shock had worn off, spoke of feeling liberated. Suddenly emancipated from a lifetime of material possessions, they felt strangely relieved and lightened. They felt that this cataclysmic event had given them new direction, a chance to reframe and rebuild their lives in a fresh and more focused way. They even came to view what seemed at the time to be a great misfortune as a blessing in disguise.

In October of 1999, I was giving a talk to a theatre full of people at a Humanistic Medicine Conference in Bavaria. I had used the phrase "making friends with cancer" several times when a woman in the front row became quite agitated. Apparently no longer able to contain her emotional reaction to what I was saying, she called out, "No, no, that is not right. Cancer is bad; you don't make friends with cancer." My heart went out to this woman as I tried to assure her that I was simply sharing a personal response to a particular situation in my own life.

The word "cancer" sets off such alarm in the human brain that when it lands in our laps, we tend to go numb. A cancer diagnosis can catapult us into a fear-driven unconsciousness. Our terror of dying renders us naive and compliant. We give away our power to medical professionals as the irrefutable and final authorities in how to prolong our lives; we forfeit our voices and our choices.

When something occurs which we do not like or which we perceive as unfair, our first reaction may be to retaliate, to fight back, or to attack. We are drawn into combat, almost against our will, because we have not taken the time to notice if going into battle is actually what we want to do, or if all out war is really the best or only way to proceed.

Sometimes it becomes imperative for our survival to find new ways to perceive and interpret life's challenges, to let go of old or habitual patterns in order to make informed decisions and conscious commitments in the present. There is no right or wrong answer. Each of us must navigate her or his own way through the formidable waters of something as alarming as a cancer diagnosis, whether that diagnosis is our own or has become the plight of someone we love. The crucial point, if we are to evolve as individuals, is to step back from the reactivity of our mind long enough to respond in a way that will help us move forward thoughtfully and consciously, and in a way that promotes wholeness and healing in the largest sense possible.

My intimate encounter with cancer has increased my understanding of how we empower or disempower ourselves through the choices we make in life. We have the power to choose our own response in any situation. The choices we make may not be the popular choices or the most agreed upon choices, but they must be the choices that are authentic for us. They must be the choices that empower rather than subdue us, and they must be choices for which we are willing to take responsibility.

The time to head off cancer is not when symptoms present themselves. It is quite possible that at least 60% of cancer is preventable! Research shows that diet and life-style choices can dramatically reduce the risk of getting cancer. Vigilance can lead to earlier detection of many cancers. Early detection can not only increase the chance of survival but can mean less invasive treatment options.

The time to prepare for a rendezvous with cancer, or with any circumstance that brings us face to face with our mortality, is not at the point of the diagnosis or of the unexpected occurrence. We prepare ourselves to meet such challenges by the way in which we choose to live our daily lives, and we prepare for the tidal waves of our existence by practicing on the smaller waves. The more we are able to observe the effects of our choices on both ourselves and others, the more we will grow in our ability—when faced with greater stresses, barriers, and challenges—to make effective and life-affirming decisions.

This book is not a "how to" on what to do when your life is touched by cancer, nor is it an overview of available treatments or therapeutic options. I share my small story because, in the reality of our interconnectedness, it has something to do with all our stories and with everyone's search for meaning in the events of our lives. It is my intention in sharing it to suggest the possibility of more spacious perspectives, ones that might allow us to open to those things which we fear instead of shutting them out, ones that permit us to face the darkness in our lives knowing that it has more to give us than just a deeper appreciation for the light, and ones that support our unbiased presence in the lives we have been given.

I am no longer so much concerned with the length of my life as I am with its quality. To me, the worst diagnosis of all would be an unlived life. The important query is not how long my lifetime will be in years or what I will die of. The significant questions are: Am I still growing? Am I learning? Am I loving well? Am I helping others? Am I making healthy, conscious choices? Am I contributing in some way to making the world a safer, saner place for all of us? Am I awake? Am I present? Am I saying yes to life now?

Chapter One

Cauldron of Change

When the fabric of the world begins to unravel,
the threads of our stories unwind
within the cauldron of change.

David La Chapelle

The vague abdominal discomfort and erratic bowel symptoms, along with a slight loss of appetite and fatigue, suggest I have some sort of flu bug. It is autumn, always a very busy and somewhat tense time of year in our household.

I am extremely anxious about a very stressful predicament in the life of one of my adult children. The situation is highly charged emotionally. It is not something that I have control over, yet I feel compelled to try to help. My inability to change the situation evokes in me feelings of powerlessness, frustration, anger, and sorrow. The circumstance itself delivers up issues from my own childhood in a very forceful way and from a different perspective than I have dealt with before. I feel sad, depressed, and "off center."

I reason that perhaps my lack of stamina is at least partially an aftereffect of the eye surgery which I've undergone in late August to repair a macular hole—a fairly rare visual impairment—in my right eye. The two-week facedown positioning required after the surgery in order to insure the best possible outcome, was hard on my body and even harder on my psyche. I naturally lost a bit of weight and

Snapshot taken four months before cancer diagnosis

strength during this period of inactivity and subsequent readjustment to an upright position.

When my digestive symptoms continue into November, I call and make an appointment with the medical doctor I've seen a few times before within our HMO (health maintenance organization—a pre-paid medical insurance plan). I write down each symptom and how long it's been occurring. The doctor reads my list and suspects some gastrointestinal problem. He prescribes Tagamet and refers me to the Gastroenterology Department of the medical center, also ordering a sigmoidoscopy and a blood work-up. In addition, I ask him to check a spot I've discovered in my lower left abdomen. It feels like a hard lump and there is no corresponding spot on my right side. My massage therapist, my husband, and I have all felt it but it seems to come and go; I can't always locate it. The doctor says he feels nothing unusual there. Perhaps I'm just being an alarmist. If the doctor can't find it, perhaps it isn't actually there, or so I want to believe.

The blood test results show that I am anemic. I am put on massive doses of iron and sent back for additional blood tests. The cause of the anemia is the puzzle the doctors set about to solve.

In mid-December, after years of working full time and going to school at night, my oldest daughter is graduating from college with high honors. Though I am filled with pride and joy for her accomplishment, I can barely celebrate. Eating is becoming less and less pleasurable as almost nothing appeals to me. I push myself through the days, going through the motions of preparing for the holidays when, for the first time in my life, I have little interest in baking, singing, or decorating. I have to force myself to eat anything and I am losing almost a pound a day.

The sigmoidoscopy (examination of the sigmoid colon using a flexible viewing tube equipped with a light and camera) is scheduled for December 24th, Christmas Eve day and my husband, Barry's, birthday. I protest having the procedure done on this particular day, but he—even more focused than I am on "fixing" my health problem—insists on us keeping the Saturday morning appointment.

Enemas are required. My bowels feel quite empty by the time we arrive. I am glad the doctor who will perform this intimate procedure is female. She seems extremely competent and is also kind and compassionate. She even lets my husband come into the room to hold my hand and watch on the video monitor. I watch too—fascinated by the clean, pink tunnel that is the inside of a part of my body—until my eyes shut against the discomfort I'm experiencing. I open my eyes again to look at the little thumb size bump she says is a polyp, saying cheerfully, "Nothing to worry about, highly unlikely to be cancerous but we'll take a sample just to be sure." I breathe a sigh of relief when the doctor says the exam is over, forgetting that what has gone in must also come out, and that all the turns in the tunnel must be maneuvered not once, but twice in this procedure.

I live through the next few minutes only to be told afterwards that I will now need a colonoscopy (examination of the entire colon through an even more flexible viewing tube) in order to check more thoroughly and to remove the polyp. I do not figure out until much later that the reason a sigmoidoscopy is always ordered before a colonoscopy has mostly to do with the fact that it costs less. The day after Christmas I begin three days of dietary preparations leading up to the colonoscopy on the 29th.

The night before the procedure I experience "Go-Lytely" for the first time. Just seeing the word brings an unpleasant sense-taste to my mouth even now. I am required to drink four quarts of a clear liquid that tastes like sea wash in the space of one hour. After two quarts I hit a wall. It seems to me I cannot possibly swallow any more of this stuff nor can I believe that anyone else has ever actually done so. With my family cheering me on and licking a peppermint candy cane between each downing, I manage to finish all but two glasses, which I have been advised to save for the following morning.

The colonoscopy instruction sheet states, "You will start going to the bathroom within 1-2 hours of drinking the Go-Lytley." I use the one hour reprieve to gather reading materials, stake out the most comfortable toilet seat in the house, and wonder how soon my particular bowels will respond and with what force and frequency. I have no mentor in this process. It is completely new and uncharted territory for me.

As it turns out, my particular body is fairly slow to respond. When nothing has happened after two and a half hours I wonder if I've done something incorrectly and why my reaction time is slower than average. Everything comes out eventually, more than I ever imagined could be contained in those little curved tunnels I have recently surveyed. I get little sleep during the night, and by morning I am feeling very clean and very thin. The instruction sheet tells me I can have only clear liquids until after the procedure, which is scheduled for 3:30 p.m.

This medical trick is more "high tech" than last week's was. My husband is allowed to be with me in the pre-procedure room where I wait in a hospital bed. A middle-aged man occupies the space next to us and an older man and his wife are across from us. The older man is wheeled out. His wife fidgets and reads a magazine. The nurse in charge of the room chats amicably with the man in the bed next to us who seems groggy. It becomes apparent he is not a first-timer to this experience and that he has an acquaintanceship with the friendly nurse in charge who ingratiates herself to me by getting the IV needle in my arm on her first try. The older man is wheeled back into the room. His wife asks how it went. He says in almost a whisper that is nonetheless heard by all in the room that "They didn't do anything," whereupon his wife rushes over to the nurse demanding in a loud voice, "Why didn't they do the procedure?" The nurse smiles and gently assures her that the procedure was done, and that it is just the drugs talking.

The middle-aged man keeps asking where his wife is. The nurse goes out, presumably to find her. When she arrives, the nurse gives them both what is obviously bad news—more tumors were found in his colon. My husband and I feel like voyeurs and try to put our attention on something else. However, we cannot help but overhear their conversation. The palpable anxiety and fear, which the nurse's words have produced in this man and his young wife, galvanize our attention.

The nurse comes to wheel me out. Apparently I am also slow to react to the sedative that is given almost as soon as I arrive in the smaller procedure room—recalling the discomfort of the sigmoidoscopy, I do not mind receiving something to take the edge off this time—so the doctor instructs the nurse to give me a bit more as he begins his work. I see the now familiar pink tunnel on the video screen and then... nothing. I "wake up" twenty minutes later back in the larger room with my husband beside my bed. I feel no discomfort. My mouth is moving slowly. The doctor comes in shortly to tell us that what they thought was a polyp is not a polyp. He doesn't really know what it is. He's taken another biopsy. The rest of my colon looks fine. It is dark by the time we go home.

The biopsies taken are negative. I am scheduled for an endoscopy, another procedure that involves flexible tubing. An endoscope, containing a fiber-optic viewing system complete with a light source and special instruments capable of clipping tissue samples, cauterizing bleeding vessels or stretching open strictured areas, is inserted through the throat into the stomach and small intestine. Discomfort is minimized through the use of Xylocaine sprayed on the throat and a relaxant, such as Valium, administered intravenously. Once again I sign a consent paper which includes warnings about risks and complications that can occur in the procedure. Once again there seems to be no problem.

Sitting in the kitchen, looking out the window, I realize how tired I am only a few hours into the day. I feel as if something inside my body is consuming my energy and that it is not going to stop. I feel a palpable and increasing weakening in my physical being. For the first time, I have the thought that perhaps I have cancer. I say out loud, "Something is seriously wrong with me."

The next day I call the endocrinologist and ask why they haven't tested for parasites. Even though I haven't been to a third world country, I was in Europe last summer, and I have heard of people getting parasites without even leaving home. She agrees that we should test for parasites. She explains that a specimen must be sent away to an outside lab and so it takes a couple of weeks to get the results. She goes on in a reassuring voice, telling me there are other tests that can be done as well. She says, "Don't worry, we'll keep testing until we get to the bottom of this. We will find out what's wrong."

I wonder how many tests my body can endure. I know of someone who went through two years of testing, never found out what was wrong, and eventually got better. My mind rebels at the thought of more tests and I begin to fantasize about what these tests might entail and how long it may take to "get to the bottom of this."

My best friend keeps assuring me that I don't have cancer. I want to tell her she can't know that, we can't ignore the possibility that I do have cancer, until finally I realize that she is trying to reassure herself. If it turns out that I have cancer, that means that she might one day have cancer. It is too threatening.

My husband begins researching my symptoms in the medical encyclopedias and on the Internet. The endocrinologist says it could still be Irritable Bowel Syndrome and that her best guess at this point would be Crohn's Disease. From what we read, the former would be much preferable to the later. The doctor now puts in an order for a CT Scan (computed axial tomography) to be done as soon as possible. The soonest available appointment is on New Year's Eve day at a facility in a nearby town, not the medical center we are used to.

I receive a new instruction sheet; this one is bright yellow. I am so thankful I don't have to drink a gallon of Go-Lytley for this test that I do not complain at all about the smaller amounts of metallic tasting

"Readi-CAT" I must swallow at regular intervals before the procedure.

The special x-ray tube is housed in the Diagnostic Imaging Department. A soft-spoken, slender man comes to get me in the reception area. He accompanies me down one long corridor, and then another. He asks if I have a tampon in. I must have missed this directive. He hands me one (he obviously keeps a supply in his pocket) and explains that they need it as a marker in reading the scan. He comes to get me right on cue as I emerge from the bathroom. He then asks if I am wearing any metal. Since I have a zipper on my shirt and metal hooks on my bra, he shows me a cubicle where I must change into a hospital gown. Smiling kindly he now guides me into the scanning room. He manages to be sympathetic when I spontaneously register a complaint as he hands me yet another cup of barium, and says as if maybe it doesn't really matter, just to drink what I can. I dutifully down the entire cupful in one breath. He then helps me step up and onto a cold, hard, metal table and places a pillow under my head. It feels as uncomfortable as the futuristic beds look in the Sick Bay of old Star Trek shows.

I see my father lying flat on his back on the sterile silver table, appearing small and isolated in the massive machinery. I am standing in the "booth" with the technician, watching through the glass wall. I hate the fact that my father is going to die sooner rather than later and that stopping smoking twenty years earlier has not stopped lung cancer from invading his body. He looks pale and weak but he is still my hero and I don't want to be alive in the world without him.

A doctor, distinguishable as such by his white jacket, the stethoscope around his neck, and his rushed manner, is called in to put the IV in my arm. He seems preoccupied and mumbles a cursory greeting without making eye contact with me. He tries once, twice, three times to get the needle in, all the while making disparaging remarks about my veins, acting as if his inability to hit the vein is my fault. He seems quite offended when, in a feeble attempt to lighten the situation, I remark that maybe they should call in Jesse, the phlebotomist in the lab who has gotten the needle in that very vein on his first try every time I've seen him. The doctor finally moves to a different vein, gets the needle in, and quickly leaves.

The thin man places my arms above my head and disappears. I am greeted by a woman's voice over a loud speaker. She leads me through a practice session, holding and releasing my breath without moving, in coordination with her verbal cues and the red and green lights on the machine. I try to concentrate on doing exactly what I am told and the procedure begins. Just when the exercise seems endless and my arms feel numb, I hear the bodiless voice declare, "Okay that's it." The thin man reappears and releases me from my prison slab.

Several days pass. My abdominal discomfort is still vague and erratic. There is no specific place where I can pinpoint pain—it seems to move around. Only once does it occur to me that something might be wrong with an ovary. I dismiss it, maybe because I simply don't want to "go there," but ostensibly because, according to the book I consult, I have few of the risk factors (a primary relative with this cancer, never been pregnant, trouble conceiving) and few of the symptoms listed (abdominal extension, bloating). I have all the symptoms listed for colon cancer except blood in my stool, and then that, too, occurs. In my heart, I think this is the most likely answer, even though nothing was seen in the colonoscopy.

While waiting for the CT scan results, I give a three-day training workshop at the care facility where my daughter is the assistant administrator. Even though my energy is way below what it normally is, it feels good to be focusing on something other than my own weakness, and to be earning a little money. It also gives me a chance to spend some time with my first-born child and saves me a daily commute while teaching.

As I am drifting off to sleep, the phone rings in my daughter's apartment. I hear her voice soften, "She's doing okay but she's really tired. She just doesn't want to eat much, nothing appeals to her. She had a hard-boiled egg and some mashed potatoes for lunch." I hear the concern in her voice and the thought arises, so it has come to this, my family whispering about me while I sleep.

The next night, my eleven-year old is snuggled up against me in bed when the telephone rings. "It's a doctor!" she says, passing the phone to me. It's 8:05 p.m.

Dr. Chan is courteous, clinical, and to the point. The scan shows a 10c pelvic mass, affixed to something, perhaps the right ovary. It is displacing the bladder. I should see an OB/GYN (obstetrical gynecologist) right away. They will try to arrange it for tomorrow and call me. Trying my best to speak normally and to sound calm and unperturbed so as not to alarm my daughter, I ask, "Are there alternatives?" meaning are there various explanations for the findings. He replies, "An oncologist will explain the options, usually chemotherapy or radiation." My face seems to freeze as I attempt to stop the hot tears that spring to my eyes from overflowing. Suddenly my husband is standing beside the bed searching my face. "Oh, well thank you so much for calling," I hear myself say cheerfully, handing the phone back to my daughter. Knowing she is already worried and that her innocence may soon be shattered, I desperately want her to have a good night's sleep. I finish reading the story and wait until she's tucked into her own bed to let the psychological dam holding back my emotions burst open. My husband and I hold each other and our tears mingle together in the darkness.

I receive a phone call the next morning with an appointment time—obviously an add-on as it's late in the day—to see a gynecologist. I despair somewhat when I realize it's the same doctor who, a year before, tried to convince me to start hormone therapy for menopausal symptoms immediately, and implied that I was uninformed and foolish to harbor any thoughts to the contrary. He had gone so far as to say that there was no controversy among enlightened doctors on this issue and certainly no doctor in our medical system would have anything different to say. He'd had no interest in seeing any book or article that might present a different point of view or in discussing the subject further.

When we arrive at the appointed time we are the only ones in the waiting room. The receptionist, speaking English with a heavy accent, provides some comic relief, when—apparently assuming I'm going to have a hysterectomy—she pulls us aside and exclaims excitedly, "Let me tell ju, ju don have to have a scar. The doctor is wonderful, he did my surgery, he has a great technique. Let me show ju." With no embarrassment whatsoever, she pulls her sweater up over her very large stomach and pushes down her slacks to reveal two tiny scars which are, indeed, barely noticeable. "It is wonderful, no? So ju don worry about the scars!"

As we wait for the doctor, my husband asks if I have any anxiety about a scar after surgery. "No," I laugh, "that would be the last thing on my mind right about now." He assures me he has no concerns about the scar, adding that he thinks it might be kind of sexy. When the doctor enters the room the first thing my husband says is, "We aren't concerned about how big the scar is." I smile still, remembering the moment.

The doctor—whom we discover has recently undergone heart by-pass surgery and now only works part-time—seems to have transformed his personality since my last meeting with him. In this context, at least, he seems unhurried, kind, and gentle. During the obstetrical examination, never a particularly pleasant procedure, he confirms his encounter with a large, hard, pelvic mass, which we still cannot feel from the outside. He says that it could be ovarian cancer or it could be a benign fibroid. Surgery is the only way to tell. He doesn't quite see how all my symptoms could relate to this finding. He will speak to Dr. Chan. He can do the surgery in two weeks and wants to have an urologist present because it will be complicated with my bladder displacement. I say I would like to get a second opinion. He says that of course he understands. In the meantime he orders a blood test to measure a substance in the blood called CA-125 which can be present in women with ovarian cancer and is thus known as a tumor marker. We try to figure out where to go for a second opinion.

The next day the doctor I have seen barely 14 hours earlier, calls to say he's referred me to a pelvic tumor specialist for a second opinion. He has telephoned all the other Bay Area hospitals who are part of our particular health care organization and has located the gynecological oncologist who can see me most quickly, even though it's a bit of a drive. This doctor is already reviewing my case and his office will call me. Things are suddenly moving much more quickly.

The doctor who performed my Sigmoidoscopy exam calls the following day to ask how I'm doing and to make sure I've had a pelvic exam. I wonder if she's feeling guilty because what she thought was a polyp was actually a tumor pushing on the outside wall of my colon. I ask her directly if she thinks the tumor is cancerous. Choosing her words carefully, she replies, "The scan was very powerful... the size is worrisome... about four inches, it's about the size of an orange." Then, apparently feeling the need to say something more positive, she adds that the report didn't specifically say "suspicious for malignancy" which they sometimes do. I ask more questions. She thinks all the symptoms are connected. She remarks that, "Lightning doesn't usually strike twice." She then tells me that she is sure I'll have a biopsy before surgery. "You will want to know because you need to make different plans depending on the outcome." My mind reels at the thought of another test, which does not, in fact, occur.

I call for the results of my most recent tests. My Pap smear is normal. My hemoglobin is 10.2; the CA-125 marker is in the normal range (21). Other blood tests, whose significance I have not yet learned, are normal.

My husband is ebullient. I don't allow myself that luxury. I have heard about false positives and false negatives. I have read that the CA-125 marker is not always present even when ovarian cancer is. As a reality check, I call an advice nurse and ask if the results of this test mean for certain that I do not have ovarian cancer. She stops just short of saying yes, though she does reply without the caveat I'm expecting, "Well, that is very good news. I would be happy with that result. I think you could certainly relax a bit."

Soon I receive a phone call from the gynecological oncologist's office. His nurse gives me an appointment time for later in the week along with directions to the hospital. One of the questions I ask her is how long I might expect to be in the hospital after surgery. I hear her say, "For ovarian cancer? Oh usually seven or eight days." Trying to swallow the lump that has suddenly formed in my throat and thinking perhaps the doctor has already reached a decision in my case, I say, "Isn't it still possible that the tumor is not cancerous?" She replies, "Of course one can never know for sure until the biopsy." It is clear to me that the doctors believe my tumor to be cancerous.

My husband chooses to remain optimistic. I contemplate the possibility of dying sooner than I'd hoped. Over the years, I've learned that ignoring a fear only makes it grow larger. Usually, the way I am eventually able to get past whatever I'm most afraid of and move on, is to let the fear penetrate my consciousness. I bring it in, think about it, visualize it, exaggerate it, imagine the worst outcome possible. I do this over and over again until the thought—in this case my death—begins to lose its power over my mind.

The doctor we've been referred to is also the one who will perform my surgery, if we so choose, and turns out to be head of the department as well as a teacher at a well-known medical school nearby. We wait only a few minutes to meet him and yet he apologizes for the slight delay! He has impeccable manners and a firm handshake. His pelvic exam technique is by far the gentlest I've ever experienced.

Once in his office, this physician/surgeon makes us feel as if he has all the time in the world for us. He speaks in a calm, slow voice, with the slightest hint of a southern drawl, giving us time to digest what he says and then asking if we have any more questions. He manages to convey the feeling that nothing is more important in this moment than our conversation—something I've not experienced in a doctor's office in years. Apparently he has not heard of, or chooses to ignore, the patient acuity study that declared any more time than three and one-half minutes per patient would result in a service reimbursement loss for the organization. The doctor listens thoughtfully, without interrupting. He is careful not to evoke false hopes or give ambiguous answers. When we run out of questions and feel certain that we want him to perform the surgery, he says it should be done as soon as possible and consults with his nurse to get me on his schedule.

My husband is thrilled because this doctor seems knowledgeable and confident as well as kind. I am thrilled because he is able to make eye contact with me and keep his attention on me during our conversation. I feel as if this gentlemen who will soon be cutting open my abdomen and becoming intimately acquainted with the inside of a very personal part of me actually sees me as an individual. This helps me make the decision to entrust him with my body.

I am given the choice between having the surgery in about a week with the understanding that a nurse's strike is scheduled and I may have to be moved to another hospital in the middle of the recovery period, or waiting an additional week to ten days. We decide on the first option. Arrangements are made for us to stay and complete most of the "pre-op" procedures, given how far away we live.

Someone gives me a poem, which I tape on my mirror where I can see it every time I comb my hair or brush my teeth.

> *All shall be well.*
> *And all shall be well.*
> *And all manner of things shall be well...*

> Julian of Norwich

I begin taking the extra vitamins, which Dr. Andrew Weil recommends people use in preparation for surgery, as well as recommended homeopathic supplements. I meditate on love. I begin creating prayers and affirmations. When I am satisfied with their wording, I make copies for a few close friends and family members.

Our therapist friends have all advised us to have our youngest daughter with the rest of the family on the day of my surgery. However, she has a fever and signs of the flu so her grandmother comes to stay with her instead. My two older children meet us at the hospital.

We sit in the waiting room together, much as we have at airports until an airplane departure disperses the group. I put my attention

on my family, sense their concern and their uneasiness, and I discern how much they love me. The butterflies in my stomach are fluttering wildly and then come unexpectedly to rest. I experience a few moments of unanticipated, precious, and exquisite peace. It's as if I have found the eye inside the storm.

The possibility that I have cancer has thrown us, all together, into a boiling cauldron of our attachments, desires, hopes, and fears; yet I feel our souls entwined in a

Snapshot of my three children

citadel of eternal love so strong that in this moment I feel completely safe and nothing else matters.

I focus my thoughts one last time on the prayers and affirmations I have created for this particular event, asking my husband and children to read them as well:

I **ask** *that the surgical team remain alert and conscious and perform to the best of their abilities to assist me (Dawn) safely through this procedure.*

I **affirm** *that the surgical team will remain alert and conscious and perform to the best of their abilities to assist me (Dawn) safely through this procedure.*

I **ask** *to (that Dawn) remain consciously open to what this experience and this tumor—whatever form it may take—have to teach me (her).*

I **affirm** *that I (Dawn) will remain consciously open to what this experience and this tumor—whatever forms it may take—have to teach me (her).*

I **ask** *that I (Dawn) may heal well from this procedure and that I (she) may accept the support and help that is offered to me (her).*

I **affirm** *that I (Dawn) will heal well from this procedure and that I (she) will accept the support and help that is offered to me (her).*

I repeat the last phrase I have written as I am being wheeled into the operating room. I hold these words and an image of my loved ones faces in my mind until the anesthesia takes effect.

I am in good hands. I am surrendered to this process. All will be well.

Chapter Two

The Uninvited Guest

I'm the one who knows what scares you,
I'm the one who loves you best
I'm the thirteenth at your table, I'm the
uninvited guest.

                                        Marillion

"Malignant" is the one word, among hundreds the doctor speaks, that penetrates my drug-sleepy mind in the surgical recovery room. It keeps flashing on and off like a red neon sign in thick gray fog. The only other word I remember for certain, a few hours later, is "chemotherapy." The weeks of waiting, weakening, unrest, and uncertainty are over. Finally, the condition has a name and the doctors, at least, have a plan of action.

I imagine my family hearing the words "ovarian cancer" from the surgeon, in the private room where they take people who are likely to cry when the doctor speaks. I feel their stomachs tighten, see tears well in their eyes, spill down their faces, and mingle together in a river of love for me and for each other. I see the beauty of that love, streaming out of each heart like colored ribbons, encircling them, strengthening them, and making the news more bearable. I feel my husband break after all the weeks and days and hours of waiting, and I know that he will put himself back together again to be there for me.

In the instant you are told you have cancer, your whole world changes and nothing is ever the same again. You think about cancer, you read about cancer, you dream about cancer. You watch yourself, and those who love you, react to the actuality of the diagnosis in varying degrees of denial, anger, fear, sadness, acceptance, and compassion.

For six days and nights at least one family member stays in my room, giving me an anchor amid the shifting sea of hospital workers who take care of the patient, yet seldom see me, the person. Few call me by name. Most focus pointedly on their assigned tasks and hurry on to the next bed. When it takes forty-five minutes and three different people to get a new IV into a vein, no one thinks to reassure me, ask how I am doing, or apologize for the extra needle sticks.

My daughter, the new college graduate, advocates for me, takes charge, goes out to the nurse's station to get whatever she thinks I might need or want. If no one is there, she finds it herself and brings it back, disregarding whatever rules and regulations govern here. Then, she gingerly places herself next to me in the bed and takes hold of my hand. Her hand still feels small inside of mine. Surrendering to her exhaustion, she falls asleep beside me.

One night I am startled awake, sweating, angry, confused. My heart is an erratic drumbeat inside my tightening chest. My breath seems to catch and stop in my throat.

Doubt and anxiety attack my reason. Hot tears sting my face as I spit out my fears in sentence fragments. My son gently, tenderly wraps me in his strong arms, holds me, and listens. Wise far beyond his twenty-eight years, he speaks to me calmly, softly, rationally. His clarity and his compassion ease my panic and quell my tears. He sits quietly beside me until I fall back asleep. In the morning he arranges all the flowers just so, turning them into a beautiful garden which nurses stop to admire.

My husband, so good at doing, at taking care of business, completes whatever task is needed. I feel his love and his fear clashing with his will to make things be the way he wants them to be. He makes the hour-long drive home once again to bring our youngest child to the hospital, because eleven-year-olds need to be included, and because we want her with us. When she sees me, I feel her longing for me to be the same as she remembers, not different, not sick, not weak and unfamiliar. Shock robs her brain of oxygen. She smiles bravely as she slips to the floor, fainting in her fear.

Of the twenty or so people attending to my post-surgical needs here, only two have looked at me and called me by name, only one has actually put his attention on me as an individual. Everyone else seems intent on doing the particular task assigned to him or her and moving on as quickly as possible. John, a nursing assistant, doesn't really spend more time with me than the others, he simply sees me, and touches my body in a conscious, care-full way. The quality of his attention makes things seem easier for the moment. It lifts my spirits. It makes a difference! When I express my appreciation to him, he puts his hands together as if in prayer for a moment and bows slightly, seemingly surprised and moved that someone has noticed his effort.

The surgeon makes his last visit, offering detailed information and answering all questions in a steady, calm, and practiced voice. Though microscopic cells were found in the abdominal fluids tested, the cancer seems not to have spread to other regions of my body. My particular type of cancer (clear cell, which makes up only 10% of all ovarian cancers) is more aggressive than some and does not always respond as well to chemotherapy. Yet "without chemotherapy there is almost a 100% chance that it will come back."

The doctor continues, detailing the well-known effects of chemotherapy and mentioning others I've never heard of. "Yes," he responds gently to my youngest daughter, "she will definitely lose all her hair." Then, as if to dissipate the collective anxiety now palpable in the room, he adds, "All the side effects should be gone within a few months after the last treatment." In an effort to keep my mind focused, I silently try to calculate exactly how many months it may be before our lives might go back to the state we refer to as "normal."

Lest we forget something, my son efficiently types a synopsis of the doctor's words onto the laptop computer I brought to the hospital, thinking in my pre-surgical, pre-diagnosis innocence I would get some work done after the operation. The surgeon now makes a point of stressing that any alternative treatment should be done concurrently with—not instead of—chemotherapy. Since I will be seeing another oncologist closer to our home, this one urges me once more to begin chemotherapy immediately, then crosses the room to shake my hand, smiling warmly as he wishes me good luck. As we are left alone to ponder the fragility of life, silence settles upon our little group like a chilly mist, momentarily freezing our thoughts.

The next day we pack up the accumulated floral arrangements, photographs, and miscellaneous unused hospital room products. I am sent home—minus my uterus, my ovaries, and a section of my colon—with a fancy new thermometer and a temperature tracking log book, a brown paper bag full of plastic medicine bottles, and some booklets that promise to tell all we need to know about ovarian cancer and to answer all questions commonly asked by cancer patients and their families. In one of them, under a heading that asks, "Does Cancer Mean Certain Death?" I read for the first time that only half of the people diagnosed with cancer will die of that cancer. In another, I read that women treated with chemotherapy for ovarian cancer may have an increased risk of developing leukemia later in life.

Our home fills up with flowers, friends, food, fragrances, cards, letters, books, opinions, suggestions, and ideas. Fax and phone messages accumulate while I receive impeccable, loving, and compassionate care. I start to worry about my caregivers. Do I really deserve all this love and attention? Can I get better? Am I doing the right things? Can I tolerate chemotherapy? Will I survive? How do I deal with this entity which has come unbidden, unwanted into our home, invading my body and my life? My questions echo those of thousands of others whose peace this uninvited guest has shattered. Why me? Why now? Why?

In the middle of the night when I cry for no logical reason—feeling a tidal wave forming in the now empty place deep inside my body, rising upwards into my brain, breaking against the edges of my fear, and spewing its waters onto my face—he is there beside me, holding me tenderly, completely, with his body, with his love, as my tears wet his face, his chest, listening to me talk about my grandmother who once told me that when she found out she had breast cancer, my grandfather was working in South America, and she never even called him. She drove herself to the hospital, nearly running her car off a bridge when she hit an icy patch on the road, forcing her to stop and give herself a pep talk—"Now Mabel, get hold of yourself "— before driving on. She had her breast removed, recovered in record time, and drove herself back home. Why didn't she tell him? Was it an act of bravery or of cowardice? Was he so frail he needed protecting? When he returned did he admire my grandmother or did he feel betrayed?

Inundated with new information and pressured to make decisions quickly, I am determined to stay consciously "awake" and in touch with my true feelings. I struggle to find healing approaches which I can commit to and an attitude that will help me feel empowered instead of victimized. A few weeks after my diagnosis, I come to a decision. All the metaphors I keep hearing about fighting cancer, doing battle with cancer, beating it, and conquering it simply do not resonate within me. Though I am committed to doing whatever is necessary to regain my health, I feel compelled to find more positive ways of viewing my situation. It is not okay with me for the lingering cancer cells to stay in my body and I begin taking steps to get them out, yet it does not seem useful to me to see this cancer as my enemy. I want to learn all that I possibly can from it, for whatever time we are destined to co-exist. For me that means finding some way of welcoming the uninvited guest, finding some way to make friends with the cancer in order to learn from it, to gain something from the relationship which has been thrust upon me.

How do you welcome such a guest—an entity who has already taken up residence in your body and in your house, one who is "robbing you blind," stealing your time, your energy, your strength, your dignity, your resources? Evicting the guest may take every ounce of strength you have left, may force you to call upon resources you didn't even know you possessed.

Even though it may be what you thought you least wanted or expected, you must entertain the possibility at least, that this demon could be an angel in disguise, could be the teacher you most need. One day you may even thank it for coming. You may thank it for slowing you down, for waking you from sleep. You may thank it for ridding you of your false pride, your vanity, your extra weight, your old hairstyle. You may thank it for liberating you from your expectations and attachments, and lightening your baggage so that you can proceed on your life's journey less hampered and encumbered.

Chapter Three

Choices

The possibility of redemption, then,
lies in how we implement our choices,
how we embody in our actions
the values we hold as sacred.

Marcia Falk

It may well be that our attitude at the beginning of a difficult undertaking plays a large part in determining its outcome. Maybe that saying, "what matters most is not the cards you are dealt in life but how you play your hand" is applicable. The media is beginning to report links between positive thinking and healing in connection with diseases such as cancer. It is quite possible that certain behaviors and emotions, such as laughter and joy, actually produce positive chemical reactions in the body that can assist in healing, and that optimistic thinking protects the body against depression, illness, and premature death. Research is suggesting causal links between emotional distress and the onset of cancer. There may even be a connection between the degree to which a person is able to give and receive love and that person's ability to survive cancer.

In the days following my cancer diagnosis, I was not thinking about all those things. I was simply trying to cope with a great deal of new information, to adjust to the reality of the situation that had presented itself, and to decide how to proceed. It took a concentrated effort on my part to stay alert. The drugs I had received before and after my five and one-half hour surgery were still affecting my body. I tired quickly and my emotions were heightened. I endeavored to stay open to my thoughts and feelings as they arose and to note them without becoming attached to them, dramatizing them, or analyzing them too much. I didn't have the time or energy to read whole books on the subject of how to cope with cancer, the pros and cons of chemotherapy, or how to choose a path of treatment (and some of the best ones had not yet been written). When I felt up to it, I read or listened to ideas, opinions, and advice from others. While resting, I spent a lot of time just focusing on my breath as a calming and centering exercise. I trusted that if I could manage to remain relatively calm, if I resisted all the mental chatter and stayed open to the wisdom of my own body—to the physician within—that I would receive guidance. I trusted that at some point the best action for me to take would become clear

A couple of years ago a colleague of mine, Helen Campbell, was experiencing her third bout with cancer. This time it was in her bones. She had undergone radiation and chemotherapy and was using a walker. I received a letter from Helen in which she remarked that while home-bound she was keeping busy fixing up her spare bedroom so she could help care for her daughter's soon-to-be-born baby. She added that anticipating her granddaughter's birth seemed like a gift from heaven coming at this particular time. She said that she had come to realize that there is no use trying to understand everything—if something cannot be changed then "accepting what is" is crucial.

A few months later, Helen wrote again, thanking me for requesting prayers for her in my newsletter. She said that she was taking medication that controlled the pain from a new tumor in her spine and was grateful that she could still drive. She mentioned that she was continuing her volunteer work—teaching massage to parents of children with special needs—since this was something she could do sitting down. The tone of her letter was so upbeat and optimistic that I was truly shocked at her death only a few months later. Her memorial service was a testimonial to Helen's choice to live a life of love and joy in service to others, and with her sense of humor in tact until the moment her body gave out and freed her spirit.

A life-threatening illness can teach us so much more than simply how quickly we can or cannot get rid of it. It can have so much more meaning than just being the worst thing that's ever happened. Contemporary teachers from Ram Dass to Pema Chödrön have tried to tell us that it is conditions such as these—when that which we least expect or want to happen, happens, when our hearts are broken open, when things fall apart, when terror comes upon us—which offer the greatest opportunities for growth. It is times like these that move us through our complacency, carry us into new dimensions of awareness, and free us from our desires and attachments to things being any certain way.

In the movie, *One True Thing,* the main character, portrayed by actress Meryl Streep makes a choice—like my friend Helen—to live an authentic and full life up until her death. She makes a choice to continue helping others to whatever extent she can. She does not throw up her hands wailing and moaning that life is unfair, that she doesn't deserve this tragedy. She does not run away from her family to do something she's always wanted to do, leaving her husband to fend for himself. She doesn't shut down and hole up in her room with her own resentment. She continues to live the life she has chosen, the one that gives her joy. Shortly before her death she says to her daughter, "It's so much easier to be happy... it's so much easier to choose to love the things that you have... instead of always yearning for what you are missing or what it is you're imagining you're missing. It's so much more peaceful."

Pain, disappointment, trauma, and grief may be an inevitable part of the human condition, but a miserable existence is not. We cannot always control the circumstances of our lives, yet we have the power to choose how to respond to those circumstances. Victor Frankel's oft-quoted statement that everything can be taken away from us except what he calls the last of our human freedoms—the ability to chose one's attitude in response to what occurs—has enormous power coming from someone who survived the unspeakable horrors of a Nazi prison camp.

Our minds and bodies react constantly… to events, to what others say and do, and to our own thoughts, emotions, and perceptions. We can make a conscious choice to look at anything that occurs in a different light. A small shift in the way we perceive a thing can sometimes make a tremendous difference in what happens next, and sometimes, can even influence an eventual outcome. How we respond can make our lives a paradise or a purgatory.

There is a story told in various spiritual traditions about a man who asked his teacher to educate him on the difference between Heaven and Hell. His teacher took him to a place where there were two doors side by side. "Look inside one door and you will find Heaven," the teacher says. "Inside the other door is Hell." So the student picks one of the doors and opens it. Inside he sees a large banquet table with all kinds of artistically prepared and delicious looking food. Wonderful aromas waft through the air. Yet when he looks at the people sitting around this banquet table, they are all emaciated and sorrowful looking; they seem to be starving while sitting right in front of a sumptuous feast! The student looks more closely and notices that all the people have boards strapped to the backs of their arms. On further inspection, the student sees that all the people have forks in their hands but they cannot get the food from the table to their mouths because they cannot bend their elbows. Unable to get the nourishment they so desperately need, the people continue to moan and wail in frustration.

The student moves quickly to the other door and opens it. Inside, he sees the very same large banquet table with all the same delicious looking foods. All the people around the table have the same boards strapped to their arms, yet these beings look happy and healthy! Everyone is smiling and conversing cheerfully. Puzzled for a moment, the student suddenly realizes the difference. Instead of trying to force food into their mouths by straining against the rigidity of their arms, these people are holding their arms out straight and feeding each other!

In the throes of dealing with a potentially fatal illness, it becomes critical to rise above the dismay and apprehension that grips the mind. When fear arises, the impulse may well be to run away, yet it is in just such frightening times as these that the choice to stand still and face the fear may make the biggest difference. Spiritual teachers often say that fear is a natural reaction to moving closer to some truth.

The Japanese poet, Basho writes in his now famous haiku:

My house burned last night
Tonight I have a clear view
Of the moon

This thought represents a remarkable response to what most would experience as a tragic loss, a response that would surely require an enlightened mind. However, this kind of shift in perception is a choice open to every one of us in any circumstance.

The longer we dwell on what we do not have, the more power we give our negative thoughts. A small shift in focus can have enormous consequences and ripple effects. Focusing, for example, on abundance rather than on scarcity, can decrease stress and anxiety; give one a more cheerful countenance; lighten body, mind, spirit, and space; evoke more positive responses from others; and make normally unpleasant tasks or situations seem easier to cope with. In addition to all that, it boosts the immune system.

In my office I keep a framed photograph of a single red rose on a long stem. Below the photograph is written, "I can complain because the rose bush has thorns or rejoice because the thorn bush has a rose. It is all up to me." I reflect frequently on the implications of this assertion as I experience and observe the power that a variation in response has in terms of how we live our lives and how we relate to others.

The choice of where to focus our attention is something completely within our power. We can choose to see the light instead of the dark. We can choose to see beauty instead of ugliness. We can choose to hear the compliment rather than the criticism. We can let our thoughts dwell on health instead of on sickness, on abundance instead of on lack.

A few years ago, I fell and injured my ankle, not badly, but enough to weaken it and cause some annoying discomfort. A couple of days later I was on a family outing. As I walked from place to place that day, I began to notice that at a certain point in each step I took, my ankle hurt. Then I noticed that there was also a point in each step that I took when my ankle did not hurt. I decided to try to focus on that point instead of on the point of pain. By shifting my focal point to the space between the points of pain, I was able to walk on and enjoy the day without being bothered by the discomfort.

Forming an attachment to a thought or to a point of view will eventually lead to believing that point of view and equating it with THE TRUTH. There is always more than one way to perceive that which occurs, as illustrated by the old story about five blind men being asked to describe an elephant and basing their description on the particular body part they first encounter.

Observation offers clear confirmation that different minds react in different ways to the same events, both in cataclysmic occurrences and in everyday life. Imagine a situation in which someone enters into a room full of people at a party. As he or she walks in, that person trips and falls, knocking an expensive vase off a piece of furniture in the process. One person observing this event thinks, "What a klutz!" Another assumes the person is drunk. Someone else wonders why the hosts don't warn people about the step down into the room. Someone jumps up to help the person who fell, while another rushes out to tell the owner of the vase about its demise. The person who fell could also have a variety of responses. He or she might get angry or complain about the hard-to-see step, be concerned that someone was hurt by the flying pieces of the broken vase, turn red with embarrassment and run out of the room, or simply make a joke out of the situation and carry on with an interrupted activity.

It is normal to experience fear, anger, anxiety, and grief during times of trauma and crisis. It is part of the human experience. The important thing is not to become too attached to these emotions, not to let what we are feeling become larger than who we are, or to begin believing the thoughts that the feelings can generate.

Our fears can help us access our untapped resources and can uncover reservoirs of strength, patience, and creativity. It is often our darkest hours that release our long-held wings of courage, poised to unfold just when they are most needed.

The first significant choice I made in the aftermath of my cancer diagnosis was to accept the cancer as a teacher. I decided that if such a great teacher had presented itself in my life, I must be ready for a great teaching. I did not want to miss the lesson. I made a decision to stay open and to pay attention. I felt that to resist the opportunity I'd been given, to deny the teacher because of the form, would have made me like the person who prayed to be delivered from the rooftop of her flooded house and then told the rescue squad, the boatman, and the helicopter pilot that she would wait for God to save her.

Shortly after my cancer diagnosis, a wise friend remarked somewhat casually that I needed to make a decision. "About what?" I asked. "What do you mean?" "Well," she replied, "either way is fine, but you need to make a conscious decision about whether you want to live or not." I was stunned. What was she talking about? Of course I wanted to live!

She continued, "I mean for yourself. Do you actually want to stay here or do you want to move on? You have a tendency to just let things happen to you, but you need to make a conscious decision about this one." I was so taken aback by what she said I could barely hold the thought. I felt my mind go blank for a moment as I tried to grasp the import of her words.

The more I contemplated my friend's advice, the more I realized she was right. She had uncovered and brought to my attention a habitual pattern in my personality. Conscious, active participation and decision-making has always been more difficult for me than simply accepting what I am given, "going with the flow," and adapting to whatever unfolds. The ability to adapt is, I believe, a useful trait. However, my habit of waiting to see what happens or what someone else may do or say before I make a decision, is an unconscious fixation. In dealing with cancer I wanted to make informed and conscious decisions.

I began to consider my choices. A few weeks after meeting my new teacher, I discovered a part of myself that could be consciously decisive, imperious, implacable. I made a conscious decision to stay alive.

Yes! I do want to live, in this body, in this lifetime, as long as possible. Yes! I want to live, not just for my family, not just for my children's sake, but for myself. I want to finish the work I came to do, and I want to help others find their way. I want to learn to experience joy as deeply as I have experienced sorrow.

"I choose life, no matter what."

"I take responsibility for choosing to live, no matter what."

"I choose to live."

"I choose life, for me, for myself, to fulfill my purpose in this lifetime, to make as much progress as possible."

The words "no matter what" stuck in my mind. I began to examine this phrase by letting myself imagine circumstances that might test my decision. What if my husband dies before me? What if I outlive one of my children? What if the cancer comes back? What if something even worse than cancer occurs? What if I end up with Alzheimer's Disease or become a quadriplegic? I considered possibilities that most people might consider very positive things but which I knew I might have trouble accepting. What if I become very rich or famous or both? What if I suddenly have no problems and am just happy? Opening my mind to these various scenarios became an exercise in surrender because we cannot predict the future, we cannot know what life will bring. Yet if we are open to life, then we must be open to all of it; we must be open to any possibility.

The next decision I made was to speak the truth. In other words, I chose not to deny or hide my thoughts and feelings, not to pretend things were other than the way they were for me. I knew that my husband would listen any time I wanted to talk. I also knew that he had his own feelings to deal with, as well as added responsibilities during this momentous time. I began almost immediately to keep a journal, writing in it whenever I felt up to it or was moved to do so. Anger, grief, fear, and sorrow are powerful emotions which can promote feelings of isolation and alienation from others. I felt that if those feelings were not expressed, then their power over my mind could increase and hamper my ability to move forward.

As soon as I felt able to get out, I asked a friend to drive me to the Wellness Center to attend an ovarian cancer support group. I noticed that there were at least twenty women in the room where those with breast cancer had gathered. There were only three other woman in the ovarian cancer group on that day. Apparently the number in the group had been substantially reduced recently due to several deaths. All three women were experiencing recurrences of their cancer and I felt slightly out of place. As each of the women spoke, I began to realize that I had much more support in my life than these women seemed to have. I left with great appreciation for the existence of the group and yet feeling more depressed than supported by this particular experience.

Once I had made a conscious choice to live as long as possible and made up my mind to befriend my cancer in the sense of accepting it as part of my life and learning whatever I could from it, the pressing choice on the table was whether or not to begin chemotherapy. That decision seemed to be the most urgent and it was one of the most difficult decisions I had ever been called upon to make.

In working with the dying as a massage therapist for hospice, and through the COMPASSIONATE TOUCH® Program I had created for those in later life stages, I had seen firsthand the ravages of chemotherapy on physical bodies, the debilitating effects, the drain of energy. Several people had shared with me that if they ever had it to do over again, they would not go through chemotherapy treatments because of its erosion on their quality of life in the short time they had left to live. Others said they weren't sure the "cure" was any better than the disease.

My father had decided to end the treatments that would have almost certainly prolonged his life when he experienced the after effects of his first chemotherapy treatment. Some family members objected strenuously to his decision. I desperately wanted my father to live as long as possible, yet I felt strongly that it was his life and his choice to make.

My father-in-law rejected chemotherapy as a life-prolonging prescription for his cancer and chose to follow a controversial medical treatment option that involved travelling to the East Coast several times. He also took up a daily practice of visualization and meditation exercises gleaned from a Carl Simonton workshop which he and his companion attended after learning he had cancer. His choices seemingly extended his life for at least a few months and certainly appeared to improve the quality of his life up until his death.

My stepsister chose to go to an "alternative cancer clinic" where she received specialized treatment and learned a strict dietary and nutritional regimen to follow at home, rather than receive the chemotherapy and radiation treatments recommended by her doctors. Her health improved for awhile and then failed again. She eventually accepted a low dose chemotherapy drip, while continuing with herbal and other treatments until her death, which she truly never believed was imminent. It's impossible to know if she might have lived longer or gone into remission had she made different treatment choices.

I had long viewed chemotherapy as a very backward and antiquated medical treatment. I had always believed that if ever the choice became mine to make, I would not accept chemotherapy and would look instead for alternative treatments. My husband and adult children knew my thoughts on the subject and were experiencing their own anxieties about how I might want to proceed. My husband told me that it was my life and my decision to make. He said he would support me no matter what, and I trusted his word. At the same time, his apprehension was palpable. I found I could not ignore the feelings of my closest family members in making my decision. Most importantly, however, I wanted to make an informed and conscious decision, as those before me had done. I wanted to own my choice so that I would be able to accept responsibility for whatever the outcome might be.

It has become clear to me that if one is to live in the present and keep an open mind, it is nearly impossible to say what you will or will not do in any hypothetical future circumstance. Reality is often quite unlike that which we may have imagined. The actuality of a situation can be vastly different from our theoretical ideas, no matter how well researched or thought out those ideas may be.

Two oncologists had told us that without chemotherapy my cancer was almost certain to return within two to three years. My surgeon had added that if the cancer came back it would probably be more difficult to treat the second time around. According to the doctors, chemotherapy would cut the risk of the cancer returning in half. I asked a physician friend to check with her sources. The statistic she reported was about a 60% chance my cancer would not return if I completed the recommended chemotherapy treatments. Based on her own personal experience with breast cancer, she also presented her view of chemotherapy as a "life saver." The statistics certainly presented a fairly convincing case for chemotherapy. However, I am an individual, not a statistic. I was not yet convinced chemotherapy was the right thing for me to do.

My husband went to work researching other possible treatments for my stage and type of cancer. He discovered that within the medical profession, the current definitive or "gold standard" treatment was definitely thought to be Taxol and Carboplatin. One oncologist told me that if I had to get ovarian cancer, I was lucky to have gotten it now instead of eight years ago when Taxol—a powerful natural substance originally extracted from the Pacific Yew tree—was not yet available. We discovered that some Canadian doctors were currently using radiation to treat earlier stages of ovarian cancer. My surgeon argued that radiation can be as hard on the body as chemotherapy and that there was no evidence that the outcome would be any different using that protocol. It seemed as if I would have to find another oncologist, probably one in Canada, to support that treatment.

A friend in Hawaii faxed thirty pages of information about a center for cell-specific cancer therapy in the Dominican Republic. He knew a woman who had been successfully treated for Stage IV Ovarian cancer at this innovative center which uses electromagnetic energy to target and destroy the cancer cells without killing healthy cells in the process. Though this clinic certainly offered a more benign approach than chemotherapy, it required long distance travel, cost $30,000, and offered no better statistics in terms of recurrences than the ones we'd already been presented with. Although we might have been able to borrow the money, going into debt and being away from my family and friends for weeks in a foreign country, did not seem like a viable option to me.

I began searching for a way to view chemotherapy as a positive and acceptable healing modality. I put my mind to selecting complimentary therapies that might make the side-effects more tolerable and enhance the treatment, and to exploring adjunctive healing modalities which might support my healing. Gradually the approaches to recovering my health that felt most authentic and right for me began to emerge in my consciousness.

Chapter Four

Healing Strategies

You're on the frontier when you're
dealing with cancer.
You're on the frontier of your spirit,
of your emotional life, and of medicine.

Selma R. Schimmel

I receive a call from a friend who is an acupuncturist. She tells me that she works with another acupuncturist who specializes in treating people with ovarian and breast cancer. He is currently meeting with colleagues in China but she has taken the liberty of making an appointment for me to see him. I am convinced I want to see Dr. Cohen long before she finishes extolling this man's virtues and accomplishments. I feel grateful to her for making the appointment possible.

Many years ago I had a bad case of laryngitis in the middle of an eight-week run of a play I was performing in. A friend suggested I try acupuncture, a key component in Chinese medicine that dates back at least 2500 years. I knew that acupuncture was a method of treating disease by inserting needles into specific sites along energy meridians in the body. Since I was something close to a needle phobic it was not a treatment I had ever considered. My friend assured me that the very thin acupuncture needles inserted superficially did not hurt. Since nothing else seemed to be helping my laryngitis and I desperately needed my voice back, I had plunged through my fears and gone for a treatment. I experienced very little discomfort. I could actually feel only two of the needles after their initial placement, and so was shocked to open my eyes and see at least twenty of them protruding out of my body, including one in the spot right between my eyes! The effectiveness of the treatment was remarkable. I had regained my voice, in the lower ranges at least, enough to go back on stage the next night.

Acupuncture had more recently relieved my pain when I experienced a severe bout with tendinitis and bursitis (doctors prescribed cortisone shots) and helped me regain strength and movement after a knee injury. At this point, I feel comfortable with acupuncture as a healing modality. I don't completely understand why acupuncture works but I know that it does.

I read that the American Medical Association is now recommending acupuncture for cancer patients for both pain relief and to alleviate nausea and vomiting during chemotherapy treatment. This gives me reason to hope that, even though they have not done so in the past, our HMO might pay for acupuncture treatments for my current situation.

An Israeli by birth, Isaac Cohen specializes in traditional Chinese oncology. For the past decade he has been collaborating with American medical oncologists to design clinical trials, laboratory analyses, and research methodology for assessing the effectiveness of Chinese medicine in treating cancer. He believes that integrating the best of Western science and centuries-old Oriental clinical experience will result in clinically effective methods that can be used in the near future.

Isaac, who asks me to call him by his first name, comes across in our first meeting as thorough, knowledgeable, confident, reachable, and compassionate. He is easy to talk to and candid, ready to answer all questions. His twinkling aliveness, sense of humor, and his gentle touch inspire hope and confidence in me.

Isaac explains that if I decide to accept chemotherapy as part of my treatment, he can see me twice in each cycle. He will treat me before the infusions to help strengthen my body, and a week after the infusions to help counteract whatever side effects occur as a result of the chemotherapy. He will also give me herbs in powdered form to be mixed with warm water and taken three times a day. His fees are comparable to those of other acupuncturists I have seen, lower, in fact, than some in our area. He has experience with our health plan and believes we will be able to get reimbursed for the acupuncture treatments. I feel Isaac has the integrity and the skills to partner me in a healing process. I believe I can trust him.

Another well-known and respected acupuncturist in our area, Dr. Lam Kong, whom I and other family members have seen over the years, learns of my cancer diagnosis through his daughter, who is one of my husband's students. Dr. Kong sends word through her that he will be happy to work with me. I feel touched by his generous offer and doubly blessed that both these acupuncturists are available to me. Eventually I decide to work with Isaac because of his specialized experience in cancer treatment.

"Tell Dawn to go see this woman. Her name is Nancy Fitzgerald and here is her phone number." This cryptic message was written on the pad in my office when I returned from an errand months before my cancer diagnosis. Barbara, the woman who left the message, is a friend and a skilled massage therapist who, after many years, knows my body well. I trust her intuition and my curiosity is piqued. I make the call.

Nancy lives in a suburban neighborhood a few miles from my home. She is a parent, a wife, a teacher, a dog lover, a healer... an ordinary women who was born with an extraordinary facility for accessing human energy fields. She eventually connected with teachers in the shamanic tradition who helped her understand her abilities, enhance them, and take responsibility for them. She now works with those who feel guided to seek her out, in the tradition of the Medicine Womyn. She has studied with and continues to learn from several well-known and unknown Native American healers.

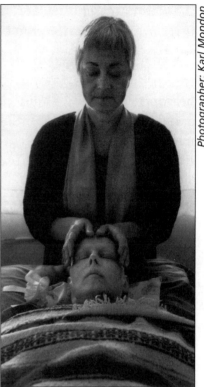

Healing session with Nancy Fitzgerald

Medicine, in the context of ancient tribal teachings, refers to life energies. In such a system, people are said to have hundreds of senses and thousands of levels of consciousness or being. A Medicine Man or Womyn works with these levels of a person's beingness or energy, those that are seen and the many more that are unseen. Nancy supports individuals in achieving balance in some of these energy fields using tools such as sound—from drums, gourds, tuning forks, and musical tapes—colors, aromas, crystals, and touch. Each tool has its own distinct vibratory rate.

I am not versed in Quantum Physics but I do know that science is beginning to prove certain things that metaphysicians have always known and that human beings have long experienced on an intuitive level. It is my own experience that is most real to me. In my first session with Nancy, I had walked in feeling like a Picasso painting and after an hour on her table, walked out feeling like a Monet. It was an impressive change. Her forthright manner, her obvious ability to effect changes in my energy, and her keen inner vision impressed me that first day. She also offered me wise counsel with food for thought.

When Nancy hears about my cancer diagnosis, she calls and offers to work with me. At our first session she helps me see that my preconceived ideas about chemotherapy are narrow and negative and gives me some suggestions for broadening my perspective on the matter. I can look at chemotherapy as one alternative in an array of treatment choices I might use in bringing myself back to health. I can think of the chemotherapy drugs as strong instead of bad, as medicine instead of poison. It is Nancy who, at the end of our second session, mentions that I need to make a choice about whether I really want to live. She also says she would be happy to see me on a weekly basis. As part of a traditional lineage before her, Nancy does not charge for her services. She is quite clear on this point. She accepts donations yet she applies absolutely no pressure, subtle or otherwise, for money to be given in exchange for her services. Her offering is unconditional. I gratefully accept her offer. I believe she has the ability to help me heal myself.

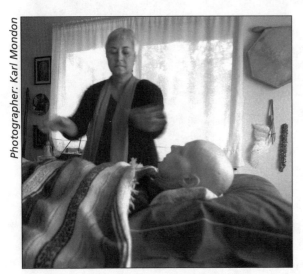

Photographer: Karl Mondon

Healing session with Nancy Fitzgerald

Nancy's expertise, wisdom, and support will become instrumental in my recovery process. Eventually I begin to both relax and feel empowered almost as soon as I step inside her session room. The space has been arranged with great attention to detail and balance. The colors are carefully chosen; each object set in its place mindfully and for a specific function. The energy of the room feels clean and clear to me.

Nancy's style is supportive more than directive. As far as I can tell, she has no preconceived agenda other than being present and being a conduit for the skills and wisdom she draws from an ancient spiritual healing tradition to support my recovery in body, mind, and spirit. Sometimes she offers a clairvoyant comment or remarks on something she observed in my body or in one of my energy fields. If I ask for it, she frequently gives me some deceptively simple and prescient piece of advice or kernel of guidance. One day she reminds me simply to love myself. "Hug your body every morning. Love every part of yourself."

I begin contemplating chemotherapy as a strong ally, which can support me in getting well. As I do so, an acrostic emerges:

Come in

Heal

Expand

Make whole

One

Much to the relief of my family, I make the decision to accept chemotherapy and call our HMO to make the appointment to begin treatments. I am told it will be three weeks before I can even see the oncologist my surgeon has recommended, much less start chemotherapy. While a part of me is glad for an excuse to put off something I dread, another part of me feels thwarted. Still another part of me feels apprehensive about waiting since delaying treatment could result in a decreased response to the therapy. I become determined not to fall victim to the system.

I telephone a physician friend and ask if she can check with her colleagues to see whom they would recommend as an oncologist within our particular HMO. When she calls me back with John Simmons' name, I realize that he is one of the oncologists on the hospice team I worked with for several years. I have an additional casual connection with him because our children attend the same school. In my newly acquired personal need for an oncologist I simply hadn't thought of the most obvious one. I call the Oncology Department once again and find he has no open appointment times for several weeks either.

I hesitate to push my advantage by calling Dr. Simmons at home, yet I feel if ever there was a time for me to be assertive, this is it. Apparently just making the decision is not enough. I must be willing to reaffirm my decision by taking responsibility for making sure I get the treatment without delay. I finally decide to risk offending the good doctor and telephone his house several times, leaving enough messages that he must realize I'm not going to give up, and finally he calls me back. When I explain the situation he agrees to see what he can do when he gets to the office the next day. He is able to facilitate my receiving the first chemotherapy infusion only a few days later at another hospital in a nearby town, and arranges for me to have my first appointment with him a week after the infusion.

The newest member of my medical support team is the epitome of my image of the kindly and harried, absent-minded professor. Though I have known him to show up an hour early at his children's school performances in order to save seats in the front row, he seems to run continuously behind schedule in work-related activities. We sit in the waiting room a full hour for our first appointment and spend another twenty minutes in the examining room before he is able to give us his attention. Once in the room, he launches into a somewhat lengthy, illustrated lecture containing information that we already know from our own research and exploration, or from direct experience.

Though staying on schedule is obviously not Dr. Simmons strong suit, he is extremely thorough, open to new ideas, and has an impressive ability to navigate the health care system. He is quite adept at cutting through red tape to procure additional information or services. Most importantly, from the very beginning, he is supportive of the complimentary therapies I am interested in following in conjunction with chemotherapy treatment. He guides us through the necessary steps that must be taken which will enable us to receive reimbursement for acupuncture. He gives me forms to fill out and tells me exactly what to do and what to say to get what I want or if I run up against barriers in the administrative labyrinth of this large medical organization. In terms of dealing with the inevitable and sometimes seemingly interminable wait in the reception area, I follow his nurse's suggestion. I learn to call ahead to ask how far behind schedule the doctor is before driving to his office, and to try to make my appointments for earlier in the day.

Like most people who have heard or read about chemotherapy without directly experiencing it, I have harbored a number of assumptions—some turn out to be accurate, some not—about what happens in chemotherapy treatment. I know that chemotherapy drugs are poisonous and highly toxic. I know that such drugs travel through the body killing cancer cells and all other fast-growing cells as well which explains some of the commonly known side effects of treatment such as losing one's hair and appetite and stomach problems such as nausea, vomiting, and diarrhea. I know that most, but not all, chemotherapy drugs cause hair loss.

I had no idea that there are many different classes and kinds of chemotherapy drugs and that each one can cause slightly different side effects, or that even the same drugs have varying effects on different individuals. I do not know that chemotherapy can be administered in many different forms—from pills to a continuous slow drip—in different dosages over different lengths of time. I am unaware that cardiac toxicity may occur weeks or even months after chemotherapy is administered and that by the time it is clinically detected it may be irreversible. I have no clue that all chemotherapy drugs are classified as high, moderate, or low in terms of their ability to contribute to secondary cancers and that the rate of development of new cancers following chemotherapy is higher in patients with certain kinds of cancers. I have a lot to learn.

I am, of course, familiar with the power of music to enhance the relaxation response and have used it frequently in this way for my own and other's benefit. I read about new research with music and sound being used to help people heal and to enhance immune system functioning. Books are being written about the extraordinary power of certain kinds of music to affect the body temperamentally, physically, and energetically. One of my close friends is a music therapist. When he moved to this country a few years ago, I was able to arrange for him to present a proposal to the hospice team I was associated with at the time and he was immediately hired as a part-time music therapist.

Stephan offers to come to the house and work with me, giving freely of his therapeutic skills. In our first session he guides me in a relaxation exercise. He then asks me a series of questions based on a meditation from Dr. Bernie Siegel's book, *Love, Medicine and Miracles*.[1] The questions he asks me are:

Do you want to live to be one hundred?

What happened in the year or two before your illness?

Why do you need your illness? What benefits do you derive from it?

What does the illness mean to you?

Ask your illness: Why are you here? What do you want to teach me?

He records my answers to all these questions, types them up later, and sends them back to me for my further reflection. In subsequent sessions Stephan helps me prepare for my chemotherapy treatments with guided visualization and meditation exercises. He assists me in choosing music to play during the treatments. I have a cassette tape of music which I first heard during a bodywork session with a healer who was happily disguised as a physical therapist deep inside the maze of our health maintenance organization. I had discovered him fortuitously during a bout with bursitis in my shoulders, which was followed closely by a knee injury. When he played this particular music in one of our sessions, it felt as if the sounds were coming from inside my body into the room. I experienced the music wrapping itself around me in a soothing caress. The sweetness of it brought tears to my eyes, dissolved my discomfort, and melted my residual resistance to healing. Stephan says this is the perfect tape to use during my chemotherapy treatments. We pick the section of the piece that elicits the strongest response in me and Stephan makes me an endless loop tape. We have several practice sessions listening to this music where I imagine the chemotherapy drugs entering my body and observe how I will receive them.

In the six weeks before my cancer surgery and diagnosis, I had experienced a steady decrease in appetite until very few foods appealed to me. I had to force myself to eat anything. One of the only foods that I really wanted during that time—and the first thing that I craved when I was able to eat again after the surgery—was miso soup. Since miso soup was not listed on the hospital menu, my family members, fortunately, found a Japanese restaurant nearby. When I came home from the hospital, this soup—in various forms— became a staple in my diet because it was the one thing that felt most satisfying, nourishing, and healing to me.

I remember reading that miso soup, eaten daily, was found to significantly reduce the frequency of some kinds of cancer in Japan. The fact that miso soup is what my body most wants now, leads me to two books by Michio Kushi, leader of the Macrobiotics movement in the United States, which have been on my kitchen bookshelf for several years. I have skimmed *The Cancer Prevention Diet* and *The Macrobiotic Way* and have recommended them as resources to a few cancer patients, yet I have never made a decision to really study or follow the diet myself. Now, sensing a drastic change in my eating habits may be called for, I begin to read these and other books on nutrition and diet from a different perspective. Among the several nutritional changes I consider, macrobiotics is the one that resonates with my mental and physical appetite, the one that makes the most sense to me; and it is the one that I believe I can actually follow and can commit to as an ongoing project.

In *Close to the Bone*, Jean Shinoda Bolen tells the very powerful story of Elaine Nussbaum, a woman diagnosed with metastatic uterine cancer. Elaine turned to macrobiotics after chemotherapy which, as she puts it, "made her weak, tired, nauseated, and bald, reduced her physical mobility and mental clarity, caused vomiting, fluid retention, bone marrow depression, and depressed her immune system."[2] Two years after changing to a macrobiotic diet, she was cancer free. In addition to reading about Elaine and other people who have experienced cancer remissions while following a macrobiotic diet, I speak with friends who share firsthand stories of the curative power of following a macrobiotic diet. Of course I realize that it is almost impossible to know or document accurately what causes a cancer remission because so many factors are involved. In addition, people who are serious about healing seldom pay attention to only one aspect of life and ignore every other aspect. They frequently change more than their diets. I also know that the most important factor in healing is the person's faith or belief that what he or she is doing is going to help, along with a person's ability to actually persist in following whatever discipline or multiple disciplines she or he may chose. Though I consider the possibility, I do not feel called to count solely on macrobiotics to cure me of cancer.

I come to understand that macrobiotics is actually much more than a diet. It is a way of life—a spiritual philosophy—that encompasses all dimensions of living. The macrobiotic way does emphasize eating whole grains and certain foods that are grown without pesticides, in season, and in one's own geographical region. Macrobiotics also recommends a conscious reorientation in regard to the way one cooks and ingests food. Macrobiotics encourages eating slowly, gratefully, and mindfully, chewing each bite until it is reduced to liquid. This way of eating not only places less stress on the digestive system but it changes one's relationship to food. Macrobiotics emphasizes other stress-reducing life-style behaviors such as maintaining a positive mental outlook and getting regular physical exercise. Other macrobiotic principles include improving one's quality of life by developing an appreciation for nature and cultivating both joy and gratitude. I renew my commitment to living by such principles and resolve to make the macrobiotic approach to diet and living a part of my recovery and healing process, and an ongoing part of my life.

Eliminating dairy and sugar in any form from my diet soon brings me into a new appreciation for the inherent sweetness in foods such as carrots, chard, and numerous squashes. By eliminating the use of dairy-based sauces and eating only foods without additives, I begin to appreciate the unique taste of each food just as it is by itself. By paying closer attention to what I eat, when I eat, and how I eat, I begin to notice how certain foods can affect my mood and how going without certain foods even for a few days can affect my energy level.

Several different friends who hear about my decision to follow a macrobiotic diet call to tell me there is a macrobiotic restaurant in Oakland I might want to check out. Then someone brings me a lunch from the place. It is delicious, nourishing, and nurturing. I persuade my family to take me there for dinner.

The Macrobiotic Grocery and Café has existed for years in a funky old corner building on 40th street in Oakland. The frame of the creaky screen door to the entrance of this one-of-a-kind establishment is painted a bright red. There is never a wait for seating. The décor is simple utilitarian; the scattered art on the walls a colorfully bizarre blend of new age cubism and funky modern. The variety of small wooden tables along with a few formica-topped ones and unmatched chairs look as if they may have been gathered from garage sales in the sixties. Many of the tables are wobbly. The yellowed linoleum underfoot is cracked and bumpy in places. In-season, organic fruits and vegetables are kept in bins lining one wall. A tiny square room in the back and one large, refrigerated unit contain all the other groceries.

Here, businessmen with attaché cases and cell phones, barefoot young women wearing long gauze dresses, middle-aged women wearing hose, heels, and make-up, gray-bearded philosophers, and bald-headed women recovering from cancer dine side-by-side. Young, old, tall, short, bearded and clean-shaven, overdressed, underdressed—every shade of human color—all are welcomed with equanimity. Some eat silently, slowly, thoughtfully, heeding the sign on the wall by the door that says, "Happy is the one who chews well." Some read while they eat, while others visit quietly. There are fresh flowers on the tables in tiny vases or saucers. A large blackboard on the wall behind the old glass and wood counter reveals the menu for the day in brightly colored chalk. The cooks names appear, sometimes with a short note to patrons or an artistic chalk drawing reminding us to remember the field workers or to focus on peace this day.

Eventually I establish a routine of eating lunch at the Macrobiotic Café twice a month after my acupuncture treatments. Sometimes I sit by myself and chew every bite of my meal 60 plus times, as purists in the field of macrobiotics suggest. It takes about one hour to eat this way, staying focused on the food, silently savoring every bite until it is reduced to liquid and disappears down the throat. Eating meditation I call it.

The menu varies and is always nourishing. One day an intriguing entrée called Sea Goddess soup is being served. It must have six kinds of seaweed in it and a few other things I'd never seen or heard of. It looks like some sacred potion brewed up in a cauldron and its aroma and taste are indescribably healing to me. I think I could survive on this abundantly rich nutritive concoction, if I had nothing else to eat, for a long time.

I agree with Dr. Christiane Northrup who says in her ground breaking book, *Women's Bodies, Women's Wisdom,* that we must all find our personal dietary truth. She speculates that most of us don't really want to make changes in our diets just for the sake of healing minor symptoms unless or until they escalate into bigger symptoms.

I do not believe that there is one right diet for every individual. We each have different body types, different genetic make-up, different physical, emotional, and energetic experiences and imprints. I make a choice to follow a macrobiotic diet as part of my recovery process because it feels right to me, because it seems to give me more energy, and because it supports me in feeling more wholly alive.

Can I really stick with this macrobiotic thing? Can I stay conscious? Do I really want to live? Over and over again, every day, I choose anew. I choose to heal. I choose strength. I choose health. I choose joy. I choose life.

I am by no means an expert on macrobiotic food or cooking. I am also not a fanatic. During my chemotherapy treatments when I feel instinctively that I need more protein, Isaac, my herbalist, concurs. Knowing he will not persuade me to eat red meat which I have not done for over twenty-five years for a variety of philosophical and health reasons, he encourages me to at least eat more fish and some poultry during this time when my immune system is being bombarded and stressed. Once, when I am craving a particular food that is not on the list of acceptable macrobiotic fare but one which my Irish ancestors survived on and which can be grown organically and locally, Isaac remarks, "Well, do you want the religion or do you want the healing?" It is an instructive statement. It reminds me to include my own inner nutritionist in my cache of teachers and healers.

❖

As a further investigation and exploration of what I might learn from my cancer, I begin a series of dialogues with my body, and record what occurs in my journal. My first set of answers gives me a great deal to work with in further contemplation.

What allowed this tumor to grow in my body?
Irreverence, disrespect, ignorance.

I'm sorry. Why this particular area of my body?
Overuse, genetic weakness.

Are there other weak areas in my body?
Lungs.

How can I strengthen that area?
Deep breathing and overall toning.

Will the cancer come back?
Not if you are vigilant.

As I continue to open to the mysteries and the messages of my physical body, strange as it seems, I begin to develop a relationship with it as a distinct and contactable entity outside of, yet somehow connected to, my self. The visual images that present themselves as I access a previously ignored inner voice in these conversations with my body are sometimes amusing. A white cell that seems to be representing my immune system, appears as a midget captain or general of some kind, in a blue and gold uniform. Sometimes he has a whistle in his mouth and seems to be directing traffic inside my abdomen. This little man in blue takes to calling me kid or "kiddo" occasionally, an expression my father and others of his generation used. He has a cheerful, friendly countenance and is always at the ready. He answers my questions, gives me reports, sometimes gives me advice or reminders to walk more or get more rest, to keep eating certain vegetables, and so on. This little icon seems able to summon, at a moment's notice, whole armies who are ready to serve in whatever ways they may be called upon to do so to support my healing.

After the first few chemotherapy infusions, I ask my body more questions and receive prudent answers.

What can I do for you?
Rest.

What do you need from me?
Cooperation.

How can I cooperate?
Listen. Take the time to listen and you will know.

How can I best honor you?
Stay alive.

It feels as if the pieces are falling into place as I continue to build my personal paradigm for healing. During this time I begin, spontaneously, to notice how much I have to be grateful for and decide to use a gratitude practice as a healing tool.

Gratitude grows from a decision to focus on what one has instead of on what one does not have. For instance, as a thought arises in me about some deficiency or discomfort, I can shift my attention to something that is available or something I can do. If I cannot get out of bed, I can be thankful for the fact that I am able to turn my head, wiggle my toes, feel the smoothness of silk, smell the fragrance of the roses. If I don't have the energy to drive to the store, I can express gratitude for the fact that I am able to cook a bowl of oatmeal, pour my own tea, see well enough to read, and to write down my thoughts. If I'm not up to a walk in the park, I can be grateful for the ability to stroll to the end of the driveway and back, to walk up and down the stairs, to fill my lungs with fresh air, to sing a song.

Each time I put my attention on my immediate environment I become aware of the rich tapestry of life that contains and sustains me. Realizing that many human beings do not have what I think of as basic necessities, I experience gratitude for the home that shelters my family and me, for the cars that we drive, for an abundance of food and water, for a quiet, clean, safe space to grow a garden and a child, for a seemingly unlimited supply of pens, pencils, paper, books, magazines, and for an endless list of tools and objects which make our lives easier and give it texture.

As I gaze out my kitchen window, my vision brings in a world of beauty. I see a multitude of gifts... flowers in a dozen shapes and colors, a bush ripe with lemons, two majestic redwoods, a fluffy-tailed squirrel running along the fence, the play of sunlight and shade on the gray-pebbled patio, the white shadow of last night's full moon, and a dozen shades of green silhouetted against a bright blue sky. I am grateful I can see. I hear the sound of an airplane in the distance, of birds chirping nearby, of water bubbling in a fountain, of the dog settling in to nap against my feet, sweet music from someone's stereo, the telephone ringing. I am grateful I can hear.

When I sit down to eat a meal, my gratitude for the food expands to include the ones who have prepared and served it and to all those individuals who had something to do with the food reaching my table and my mouth. I am newly conscious of the many hearts and hands which daily contribute to my experience of eating a meal—the growers, the packagers, the loaders, the truckers, the grocers, the clerks, the baggers... the earth herself.

When I focus my attention on my family and friends, it is like opening a treasure box and being dazzled by the brilliance inside. There are jewels and precious gems of all colors, sparkling like the sun. I see pearls of great price; I see nuggets of gold and objects of resplendent beauty for which I have no name. If I begin to examine these glorious treasures one by one, I see that no two are alike; each one is unique in size, color, texture, form, shape, and material. Some are multi-faceted, some are multi-colored, some are crystal clear, some are wonderfully dark and mysterious, and some are remarkably indescribable. It seems that the container has no bottom, for the longer I look, the more jewels I see until I begin to feel faint with the presentation of wealth.

If I put my attention on any other aspect of my life—home, work, community, nature, the universe—an infinite inventory appears. It's a bit like looking at one of those "magic eye" pictures where you see a lovely image and then, by continuing to look beyond the first image, shifting your gaze ever so slightly, another whole picture appears that you didn't see just a moment before. If you keep looking through that image, sometimes a third picture appears. After a few short minutes, I realize that I have more blessings than I can name or count, that abundance saturates my world, and that simply being alive is a wonderful thing. In the face of such abundance, to complain about anything would seem like a sacrilegious act, a slap to the face of God.

The simple act of noticing what one has to be grateful for has tremendous power over the mind. I use this process to get through difficult moments during my cancer treatment and recovery. I use it to shift my mood when I am feeling "down" or to cope with unpleasant tasks. After my chemotherapy treatments are completed, I use it in the dentist's office during a lengthy procedure called root planing—usually a dreaded experience for me due to a traumatic history of dental work. I simply spend the time I am in the dental chair silently recounting everything I can think of to be grateful for. By putting my attention on something other than my anxiety or discomfort, the time seems to pass more quickly; I need no numbing anesthetic, and I leave the office feeling positive, cheerful, and incredibly fortunate!

I remember a woman in a skilled nursing facility in Nevada City, California. Her name was on the list of residents who had volunteered to be seen by a student in the COMPASSIONATE TOUCH® Training workshop I was giving, during our on-site visit. I was told she had been a schoolteacher and was injured in a horseback riding accident a few years before. A quadriplegic, she was probably in her mid-thirties when I met her. This thin woman's mobility was severely limited and her primary living space was a cramped wheelchair, yet her spirit seemed as vast as the sky. As I approached her, she was reading a book, positioned on a special tray attached to her chair. She was able, with concentrated effort, to turn the pages by using a special device attached to her forehead. I remember her beautiful brown eyes that smiled even though her mouth couldn't. I asked if she had enjoyed her massage from the student who visited her. She gave an enthusiastic, affirmative nod. Then, formulating the words slowly and with some difficulty said, "Guess what?" "What?" I asked. As if she were the recipient of some great prize, her eyes sparkled when she replied, "I can feel my legs!"

The teaching she gave me in that moment was immense. I vowed never again to take anything for granted and to make every effort to rise above the pettiness of my mind in its endless complaints. Though I have broken my vow many times, I have never forgotten her shining example of positive thinking and gratitude.

It has been said that people die the way they live. In other words, a person who is bitter in life is going to face death with bitterness. A person who tries to exert his or her will to control things in life is going to be controlling as death approaches. A person who has been stoical in accepting what life brings will probably remain stoical in accepting her or his death. The person who is fully open to life is more likely to open to death when the time comes.

Occasionally I observe someone whose personality presents itself one way throughout life, exhibit a seemingly opposite persona near death. Such a change can manifest when some event occurs which the logical mind cannot absorb or take in. The phrase "that just blows my mind" is applicable, meaning that in that moment when one's mind cannot comprehend or accept what is happening, there is a blank space wherein the person is freed from a fixed state or habitual way of being.

I had a client once who was so fixated on the negative that it seemed impossible to elicit a positive response from her about anything. Bedridden for some time, she suffered from several physical and mental frailties. When I mentioned the view of the flowers through her window she complained that the light hurt her eyes. If I remarked on how pretty the room was or how the colors complimented one another, she complained this was her sister's room and said she hated the décor. If I mentioned the birds chirping cheerfully in the tree outside her window, she complained that they woke her up in the morning. When I asked how the massage on her back felt, she mumbled, "Oh, okay I guess," which seemed to be the least negative thing this woman was able to say.

I finally gave up on the idea of trying to get this unhappy woman to respond in a positive way to anything, and just accepted her as she was, doing my best to give her some comfort through touch. Her sister and primary caregiver, who had hired me to see her, eventually told me she didn't see that COMPASSIONATE TOUCH® sessions were making much difference and thought she would try something else to help her sister. I had to agree that her money might be better spent elsewhere. Much to my surprise, when I acknowledged to this client at our next session that it would be my last visit, she burst into tears and exclaimed, "I'm going to miss you!"

Some people can be momentarily distracted from their unhappy state while others chose to stay in it for their entire lives. Sometimes a person is so steeped in focusing on the negative that his or her pessimistic comments become habitual, rather than a true indication of experience.

To be sure, the decision to choose a positive response over a negative one is more difficult in some circumstances than in others. When one's body is in the throes of responding to a chemotherapy treatment is one of them. I can remember the exact moment when I understood why my father said he would rather die a few months sooner than continue with chemotherapy. As my body reacts the first time to being filled with Taxol and Carboplatin, my physical and mental capacities are so diminished that focusing on anything positive seems nearly impossible. Focusing on anything at all seems nearly impossible! Yet the moment passes, and a few days later I am not thinking the same thoughts.

Among the array of options available today, within the fields of both conventional and alternative medicines, and in the short time I've had to explore them, I have chosen a combination of healing modalities that I believe are best for me at this particular time for my particular cancer. I have opted for a multi-level approach. I have made commitments I feel I can keep.

I add some final touches in my healing garden. I make a choice to be with people whose presence I experience as healing. I choose to spend more time with optimistic, cheerful people who are enjoying life on a daily basis and less time with those who are constantly complaining, criticizing others, or wanting their lives to be different. I choose to be with people who are able to understand what a fragile and vulnerable state I am in, and who are willing to treat me tenderly. I make the choice to surrender to the healing power of love, to be open to miracles, to shut nothing out.

Chapter Five

Letting Love In

*The ability to give and receive love
includes loving ourselves.
Love is the finest energy
we'll ever draw upon.*

Caroline Myss

An immediate effect of my cancer diagnosis is a definitive shift in priorities in my life and in the life of our family. Things that seemed important the day before simply disappear from our conscious minds. Insignificant and nonessential concerns are dropped. Getting across how much we love each other is instantly more important than reading the mail or cleaning the house. Thrust unexpectedly into a state of ultra sensitivity and awareness, treating each other well, suddenly becomes a top priority. We see one another through new eyes because our status quo is threatened.

I read somewhere that opening the heart and receiving love is the best thing for someone with cancer to do. I wonder why opening to the love that I feel pouring in from others sometimes seems difficult. I resolve to let love in.

In the days and weeks following my cancer diagnosis, I am gently forced to expand my own ability to receive. The caring energy I feel directed toward me is almost overwhelming. I am not sure I can actually accept or hold it. At the same time, I know this is simply an idea, a mental construct, which I can let go of if I chose to. And so I begin, in a conscious way, to let my heart and soul open, to take in the love, to absorb it, and to let it settle in my being. I soften my mental perimeters and release my ideas about how much I can contain. I allow myself to accept the same kind of love and attention I try to give to others. I let go of the idea that loving oneself is somehow egotistical and wrong. I allow the loving energy to saturate my being. I begin to understand, on a visceral level, what has been said in many different ways by many different people that, ultimately, it is love that heals us.

As ancient wisdom says, "there is a time to give and a time to take." I decide that undergoing treatment for cancer is not a time to hold back. Instead, it is a time to "call in all markers" so to speak, and to let whatever I may have given to others come back to me. It will not be useful or authentic to avoid asking for what I most need. If I am truly to heal, I need all the help I can get!

I get my first chance to put these thoughts into practice when a student-friend-colleague offers to drive down from Oregon to help when I come home from the hospital. I say no to Willow at first. "No, it's too much. No, you don't have that kind of time." When she seems momentarily taken aback, I realize she really wants to do this, that her offer is sincere and unconditional, and that my refusal is, in a subtle way, a rejection of her. I am surprised that it takes an act of will to accept her generosity. I strengthen my resolve to let love in, drop my false ego position, and my preconceived ideas of being undeserving. I thank her for coming to help us.

Willow places herself in service to our family, quietly and unobtrusively doing everything imaginable: shopping, cooking, cleaning, laundry, taking phone messages, answering the door. She does everything else so that my family can rest or just sit with me. She gives my husband and older daughter much needed respite in the form of massage. She keeps track of who brings what and prepares whatever food sounds good to me: all varieties of miso soup, steamed organic vegetables, puddings, blender drinks. Her love and her beauty reside inside the food and her caring makes the food even more nourishing. The food is always arranged carefully and beautifully. The tray includes a tiny vase filled with fresh flowers. I weep at the artistry and my heart expands in gratitude and wonder at the pureness of such service to another. And I weep for the multitudes of valiant souls going through what I am, or with far worse scenarios, who do not have the healing gift of family and true friends in their lives.

When Willow must leave it is hard to say good-bye. She has done so much to ease me onto my healing path, has provided so much comfort, has cared for me and for my family so impeccably. It takes a few hours to adjust to the vacancy in the energy inside our home.

Soon after her departure, our "kissing cousins" arrive from Philadelphia bearing gifts of food and fashion, sharing their love, their Jewish humor, their boundless energy, their optimism, and themselves in a way that only they can. They touch me with their hands, their hearts, and their love. They take my husband out to dinner and make him laugh, and they cry with him.

Once I've chosen to accept it, the river of love coming toward me expands to oceanic proportion, flowing into my life in myriad forms. Friends in Japan share the recipe for a medicinal tea given to cancer patients there. The tea is made by chopping up some daikon and daikon leaves, carrots and carrot leaves, and burdock root which are thrown, along with a few dried shitake mushrooms, all together in a big pot which is then filled with water and boiled down to half the liquid. Our local health food store agrees to keep the leaves from the daikon when delivered, instead of discarding them, and to call us whenever they have a bunch. A friend who owns a restaurant wants to know what he can do. When I ask if he knows of a good source for shitake mushrooms, he rings our doorbell the next day holding a huge box of them! Soon I am drinking the tea several times a day. My herbalist says that in Japan this tea is traditionally suggested for people who receive radiation. He says it certainly can't hurt to take it while I'm receiving chemotherapy.

As I am looking through a directory of macrobiotic resources and teachers, I come upon a familiar name. I call the number and discover that the woman is indeed an alumnus of the private high school where my husband teaches. She was his student over fifteen years ago and remembers us both. She mentions how helpful Barry was to her during a difficult period in her life and generously offers to support us in any way she can through counseling or cooking classes.

My chiropractor, who is also a friend, calls when he hears of my situation and offers to come to the house to give me a treatment as soon as I feel up to it. My heart is touched by his generous gesture and I feel confident that the alignment will help speed my healing from the surgery. Weeks later, when I am able to go to his office, he still insists on not charging me until I am earning money again. Even though I know I would do the same thing if our roles were reversed, I find his offer difficult to accept at first and I am moved to tears by this kindness.

Queen Tootie, the nurse cat, acquiesces for the first time, allowing our two other felines to occupy space on her throne so that all three now stand guard over me like sentinels. They reposition themselves when necessary to make room for humans or food trays but they seldom leave their posts, staying with me day and night, loving me through purrs and gold flecked eyes.

My husband's colleagues put together a basket of gifts containing everything from tea to bubble bath to beanie babies for our daughter. One of his students sends flowers with a written communication sharing reflections about a loss of his own and positive thoughts for my healing. The entire senior class signs a large greeting card they have created with personal sentiments, drawings, and wishes for our family. I am deeply moved that 75 teenagers in the last semester of their high school careers are this generous and thoughtful at a time in their lives which is traditionally a very busy and egocentric one. It is a testament to their high regard and affection for my husband and to their own compassion and sensitivity.

My oldest daughter makes the hour-long drive to our house, after exhausting days as an assistant administrator in a multi-level care facility, and takes extra days off, bringing special teas, cleaning up the kitchen, and helping out in whatever ways she can think of. Often she just lies down beside me on the bed and falls asleep and I drink in the miracle of her adulthood.

Since I'm not yet up to going out, the Chavurah, a group (in this case a collection of "mixed" families interested in Jewish Renewal) we have joined less than a year earlier, come to welcome Shabbat in our home, not caring that things are in disarray or that the house needs cleaning. They bring delicious, nurturing food. They dance through the house and up the stairs, fill the room around my bed with new songs, ancient chants, and prayers that filter into my body.

Later in the evening, I make my way down to the living room in my robe and slippers. One by one, individuals come to me, touching and contacting me in unique and tender ways. The Rabbi prays over me and whispers in my ear that nothing is impossible. A length of white paper is unrolled onto our long dining room table. The children and the grown-ups gather round in ones and twos until everyone has had a turn to draw a picture or write a message—the paper is transformed as multicolored hearts and flowers and rainbows, lotus blossoms, circles, doves, and stars of David appear. People write about what helps them in times of despair or when they feel lonely or afraid. And from the last child to grow in and emerge from the part of my body that is now gone forever, emerges a narrative so precious that it shatters and restores my spirit in the same moment:

I remember the night when I found out that you (mommy) had cancer. I was so scared and afraid you would die and I didn't want to cry in front of everyone—and I know its okay to cry—and so I asked if I could leave and I went up to my room and started crying very hard. Then Brianna (my sister) came up to me and asked if I wanted to sleep with her that night. I nodded and we went down to the living room and started crying together. Soon Michael (my brother) came down and started crying with us to. Soon after, my dad came down and we were all crying together. We stayed up practically the whole night crying but I didn't care. It felt so good to have a family that was filled with so much love.

I spend hours in the coming weeks scrutinizing the poems, prayers, and pictures on this scroll, taking in the energy of the words and symbols that feed and nurture and soothe my soul, letting my heart open again and again to the devotion that created this masterpiece. Eventually I contribute drawings and words of my own, to add my energy to that of the group and to include my own symbols of healing.

Our best friends inform us that they have called a number of our mutual friends to suggest that they put their attention on me for fifteen minutes at a specific time every week. They ask me for a list of other people to call. I feel incredibly touched by this gesture. I make a conscious decision to accept this support in the spirit in which it is offered. People in other countries and time zones adjust so they can join in with the people on California time. I am told that a woman I've never met is getting up at 2:00 in the morning to take part in this healing circle.

Eventually I am able to call or write to people myself and ask them to participate in my healing in whatever form they wish to, either on Thursday nights or any other time they can. It is a strange feeling at first, asking for something for myself. However, I notice that my decision to make such a request, as well as the action of asking, make the event more real to me and add power to the supplication.

On Thursday at 8 p.m., I light a candle in the bedroom and we sit quietly on the bed holding hands. I try to let go of residual trepidation, apprehension, and fear about the future. I just surrender. Soon, the room seems to glow with a golden light. I sense the presence of beings, like the angels I saw at Meghan's birth. They were singing then. The air in the room begins to feel denser, I feel love filling up the space in the room and filling my body as well. Barry's experience is one of power surging into the room from all around us.

In the following weeks, we occasionally forget to join the circle at the appointed time, our attention occupied elsewhere. I trust that the strength of the prayer continues to work even when I'm not consciously joined to it at the particular moment it happens. More people drop into this healing circle. Whole congregations and groups of individuals, most of whom I have never met, join in. Eventually I can put my attention on the healing power this group is generating at any time, and I can pass it on to others who need the support. This incredible gift conceived of by two people, is a potent lesson in the power of prayer and synergistic focused energy.

I recall words ascribed to Jesus in scripture I learned as a child, "Ask and ye shall receive." I have direct experience, for the first time in my life, of the actual truth of this statement.

Students and colleagues come to give me massage. I find I can tolerate only the gentlest of touch during this fragile time, and only from people who can put their attention on me. If the attention is on my physical body or on the fact that I am being treated for a life-threatening cancer, the touch does not feel nourishing or healing.

Two good friends I have not seen regularly in years come back into my life bringing remarkable gifts. One, who lives nearby, comes to my house once a week for the duration of my cancer treatment and spends an hour with me. By profession, she is a therapist and so is skilled at listening without evaluating or judging or trying to change things. She asks me how things are for me and then, if I feel like talking, just listens. She accepts whatever thoughts or feelings come up for me and acknowledges my communications, without agreeing or disagreeing. This is a powerful and significant gift, in any context, and it is especially meaningful for me at this particular time. For the last half hour she reads to me from a beautiful and spiritually-inspiring book my husband has given me, knowing how much I like the 16th Century mystic poet, Rumi.

The other friend drives a distance, visiting several times during my surgical recovery and treatment. She comes bearing thoughtful gifts—the first time, a special spiral-bound notebook and a case of colored art pens for journaling and drawing. The book is immensely helpful to me in expressing and articulating in more than one form my thoughts and feelings during a time of intense emotional upheaval. It is also in this notebook that I begin to draw a Healing Garden. Each day I add another flower or some green leaves until eventually every inch of space is colorfully covered.

My 11-year-old daughter is quite interested in what I am doing in this journal. I let her look at it from time to time. I give her another beautiful book, which a thoughtful friend has sent me. I tell her this can be her own journal. I share my colored pens with her, encouraging her to write and draw as well.

On another visit the friend who brought the journal and pens announces that she is going to clean out and organize my refrigerator. She informs me I can help her by sitting nearby and telling her what to keep and what to throw out. I imagine that only another woman could begin to understand what a needed and appreciated gift this is. She provides additional healing in inducing me to laugh (which I am just beginning to be able to do without discomfort as my stitches heal) by educating me on the shelf life of various condiments which have obviously been in my refrigerator for years if not a decade.

My closest friend shows up one day with her one-year-old, her baby sitter, and her new vacuum cleaner in tow. I'm not sure which woman is vacuuming and which one is entertaining the baby, but just knowing my carpets are clean boosts my morale considerably.

A few days after one of my chemotherapy treatments, I am suddenly and completely overwhelmed when I realize my 5th grader is supposed to dress in Swiss attire for the presentation of her term project on Switzerland the next day. I take a deep breath, pick up the telephone, and call one of her friend's mothers. I don't know this woman well but I do know that she is organized, efficient, and generous. She gladly takes on the task of outfitting my daughter and tells me not to give this particular problem another thought.

I watch a television interview with a woman who has lived with cancer far beyond her doctor's expectations. The cancer has never left her body but she has been able to prolong her life through a series of various treatments, and she and her husband are writing a book about how to prepare for death. She is making a series of videotapes for her young daughter to watch after her death, including advice she thinks will be helpful for her child at various stages on her way to adulthood. During the interview, this tenacious woman mentions that she and her husband—upon the advice of a counselor—got a puppy for their daughter. The thought was that she would have an animal friend to confide in and to help comfort her in the likely event of her mother's death.

The parents' comment about the puppy sticks in my mind and makes me think that perhaps I need to relent on my resolute position in response to years of supplications from my daughter and my husband for a dog. Why should my reluctance count for more than the yearning of two-thirds of the household? Why should I deny these two people whom I love so much something they want so much? Though I have many rational objections and considerations, I open my mind to the possibility of a new addition to our family. The opening expands to a search that leads in directions I would never have imagined.

The day after my third chemotherapy infusion, we drive to a small town in northern California, spend the night in a motel, and return the next day with a much-loved and well-trained 13-month-old Bernese Mountain dog. Friends ask why now and why such a big dog? Since the decision did not arise from logic, I am hard-pressed to offer a sufficient explanation, to myself or to them.

Whitney

The answer to an unspoken prayer,
a whispered wish,
she sits at my feet in silent reverie;
and I suddenly understand
that her presence here
is no accident.

A new friend a teacher perhaps
an angel in disguise,
I am grateful
and a little scared
of the enormity of the being and
the call to expand, to grow, to open
to love, to life, to Grace.
Her beauty stops my mind,
moves me to tears and then
I don't know why I am crying
and she doesn't care.
She loves me with her eyes
asking me for nothing.
When I lie down beside her
she pushes against me
her body soft, solid, warm.
Learning my smell, tasting my tears
she licks my face and lays her head
gently, on my shoulder.

It becomes apparent to me that, in times of crisis, people do what they are good at doing, and give what they are comfortable giving. I feel encouraged, supported, consoled, and comforted during this time in unique and sometimes completely unexpected ways. One couple leaves singing messages on the answering machine or a gift on our doorstep—a cassette tape, a crystal, a flower—on the morning of each one of my chemotherapy sessions. A woman I have not actually seen in years sends me a beautiful card every single week during my six months of treatment. A relative in the east calls a wig shop in our town and leaves her charge card number, insisting I go pick out any wig in the shop I want, whenever I feel ready.

A few individuals simply inquire how they can help and actually mean it! These rare champions do whatever is needed, whether it's going with me to an appointment, driving me to a support group, searching out a book for my daughter to read about the challenges of having a parent with a life-threatening disease, helping me shop for new clothes because my old ones don't fit any more, or just listening while I untangle my thoughts. Help is available. It is up to me to ask for what I need. Love is available. It's up to me to let it in.

I resolve to pass along the generosity coming my way when I am able to do so again and when the opportunity arises. A friend tells me that at birth her younger daughter needed surgery to survive. It was weeks before they were able to bring their new baby home and during that time many friends kept them supplied with food so they could be at the hospital or with their other daughter. She tells me that she has been waiting five years to repay that kindness and that we have done her and her husband a great service by allowing them to be part of the group that is keeping us supplied with food during my recovery and treatment period.

I also come to understand that sometimes, when a person hears that a close friend or relative has been diagnosed with a life-threatening disease, the actuality catapults him or her into a kind of shock or denial such that the person is simply unable to offer help or solace. The man my father called his best friend never came to see him in the hospital after his cancer surgery, nor did he attend his funeral. Though I never met this man and his wife, my father had spoken of them many times and talked about various activities that they had shared. I felt angry about this man's withdrawal from my father in the last year of his life. I could not understand such seeming insensitivity and lack of support. I don't know if my father ever understood and was able to forgive him. I recognize now that the situation was just too threatening to my father's friend. The thought, "If it could happen to him it could happen to me," must have been difficult for him to face, and his fear froze the flow of their relationship. I know that similar thoughts occur to several of my friends. Fortunately, for me, most of those people are able to articulate how they feel and be in contact with me anyway.

After I make the decision to accept six treatments of chemotherapy as part of my recovery program, my husband makes an extraordinary statement. He says to me, "For the next six months, I don't want you to do one thing that you don't really want to do." My first thought is that he means, "We'll manage without the money you usually bring in." The truth is, he is saying something much more profound than, "Don't worry about earning money for six months." He really means, "Don't do anything you do not want to do during this time."

I am keenly aware that many people do not have such an opportunity. I know people who must work right through their chemotherapy, radiation, and other treatments, no matter how sick or weak they feel, because the money they earn is essential to their dependents, or because they do not have financially generous relatives or savings to borrow from, or for various other reasons. I am determined to use such an exceptional gift wisely.

My husband's willingness to expend the extra energy, time, and effort in running the household and "taking care of business" during this period—which actually stretches into eight or nine months before I begin to feel anything like "normal" energy—becomes an enormous aid in my recovery. This gift of time allows my body and mind to begin healing. It allows me to sleep and rest as much as I need to. It allows me to receive my treatments in a conscious and unhurried way, knowing I can follow the natural rhythms of my body in its recovery process. It allows me time to reflect on what I might have done or not done to help create the stress that has contributed to a physical environment within my body which allowed a cancerous tumor to grow. It gives me time to contemplate ways in which I can change my life-style to make it less stressful. It allows me to engage in activities that nourish my body and my soul, and to say no to those who exact a toll on my limited energy and strength.

In the Jewish tradition, a period of time is set aside each year during what is known as The High Holy Days to be used for self-inspection, specifically for reviewing one's actions during the previous twelve months. It is a time for evaluating, reflecting, and coming back to center. It is a time to assess the extent to which one is living in harmony with the Divine, to become more conscious of ways in which one may be "missing the mark," to forgive oneself and others, and to move forward with renewed focus and commitment. This process, in Judaism, is called "T'shuvah," which literally means "returning" to who and what we are, to our true nature, to God. What my husband makes possible for me is, in essence, a six month T'shuvah. It is an immeasurable gift of love.

Chapter Six

Grit and Grace

*There is no obstacle that true grit and
Amazing Grace cannot overcome.*

Sarah Ban Breathnach

There is an African myth about a hunter and a lion. In the myth a young hunter is sent out from his village, as was the custom, to meet his lion. During the second day of his search, growing weary and fearful, he stops to rest and falls asleep. Nearby, a lion is searching for water to quench his thirst and comes upon the sleeping hunter. Thinking to devour him, the lion takes the sleeping man in his mouth. As he does so, the hunter awakes and realizes his predicament. Paralyzed with fear, the hunter keeps his eyes closed, feigning sleep. The lion, deciding he must drink first, takes the hunter and wedges his body into the fork of a nearby bush. As he does so, a thorn pierces the hunter's flesh and a tear escapes from his closed eyes, rolling down his face. Seeing the tear, the lion realizes that the man is not asleep, and that he is aware of his situation. Moved to compassion, the lion licks the tear on the hunter's cheek and then turns and walks to the spring. As soon as the lion disappears, the man frees himself from the bush and runs in a panic to his village. He begs the villagers to hide him. They finally do so, wrapping him in some animal skins.

When the lion is finished drinking at the spring, he comes back for the hunter. Finding him gone, he follows his trail to the village and calls out to the villagers, telling them that they must give him the hunter whose tear he licked, for "He is mine and I must devour him." The villagers offer the lion all kinds of gifts, which the lion refuses. Finally, they go and get the hunter and tell him that he must go out and face the lion. When he does so, the lion kills the hunter and then tells the villagers that they can now kill him for he has devoured the man for whom he had compassion. The villagers begin to dance and celebrate because they know that the hunter will be reborn with the heart of the lion.

The point of the story seems to be that all of us, at some time in our lives, must face the equivalent of our own lion, in whatever form that fearsome creature may take, and that no one can face that lion for us. Mentors may help prepare us, friends may stand by us, yet in the end we stand alone. We cannot hide nor can we escape the fact that we may be devoured. In fact, it is by surrendering and by allowing ourselves to be devoured—to be consumed by the truth of our experience—that we are transformed.

As I prepare to submit to my first chemotherapy treatment, this tale leaps forward in my memory with startling clarity. Certainly I have wandered into the forest of darkness and grappled with metaphoric beasts before. Now it feels as if I am coming face to face with the so-called King of Beasts.

Everyone is a little nervous this morning. It's chemotherapy day. Time to face my lion. Heather, an exceptionally mature and sensitive teenager, comes to pick up Meghan to drive her to school. We double check to see that we have the tape recorder and music tapes, my journal and drawing pens, my medical records, our snacks, reading material, my special pillow, and the crystal which friends left on our doorstep early this morning. Barry waits for me to be ready to take the first step—walking out the door. He patiently gives me gentle reminders of the passing minutes and finally says it is time to leave.

The drive to the hospital seems both to take forever and no time at all. We sit in the parking lot and Barry waits patiently for me to take the second step—getting out of the car. As we walk toward the hospital, I feel as if all the energy in my body/mind is moving backwards as my feet move forward. I keep pushing against the thick wall of fear and uneasiness that my mind has built around this event. I remind myself that facing the fear—opening to the heart of the fear—is the trigger that will release the grip it holds on my mind. I remember that I am not alone.

The attractive young woman at the lab gets the needle in almost painlessly for the blood test and I pray the nurse in the infusion room will be as successful. I've been told that oncology nurses are experts at getting needles into veins.

I have a thought that I should eat soda crackers while the drugs are entering my body—perhaps it will help combat nausea. We find the cafeteria. When my husband explains what we want, the sympathetic server finds a basketful of crackers and tells us to take as many as we like.

We show up at the Infusion Unit a couple of minutes before our scheduled time. I feel greatly relieved that, as yet at least, there is no one else in the room, which seems to contain about six "stations." The oncology nurse is incredibly compassionate and kind. As I sit down in one of the big, gray recliner chairs, I immediately burst into tears and then whisper, "I don't know why I am crying." Handing me a tissue, she says, "Because you have cancer and you are about to get chemotherapy for the first time in your life." Pulling up a stool and seating herself in front of me, she continues, "Your feelings are perfectly normal and it is okay to cry." She encourages us to ask questions and she answers every one. As the realization dawns in me that most of my anxiety is about the needle stick and I am able to communicate that, she takes a look at my veins and quickly assures me that she can get the needle in. Her competence and confidence ease my mind considerably.

We are shown a shelf full of videotapes—all comedies—and encouraged to watch one or two during the next three hours. The people in charge here have obviously taken to heart the ground breaking work of Norman Cousins and others in regard to the power of humor and laughter in reducing stress and helping people cope with difficult situations. Prepared to concentrate on my music tape and the affirmations that I've created, I am reluctant to distract myself. My husband reminds me that laughter is also a healing tool and that it probably isn't necessary to repeat the affirmations for the entire three hours—in fact, if my conviction and confidence is strong enough, saying them over once should be sufficient.

If, as Jean Shinoda Bolen says, "Times of crisis are opportunities for accelerated lessons in what it is to be human,"[3] my first chemotherapy treatment is an exceedingly human event for me. I try to imagine what it must be like for people who have no one to accompany them on a journey such as this one. I experience immense gratitude for the fact that I am accompanied this day.

We chose a Robin Williams, Whoopie Goldberg, and Billy Crystal special. As it turns out, however, I am able to watch very little of the movie. The anti-anxiety pills I've dutifully swallowed, combined with the "pre-medication" drugs now being administered intravenously: Benadryl, given as a preventative measure to combat possible allergic reactions to the Taxol; Decadron, a steroid to help counteract nausea; and Tagamet to counteract irritation to the lining of the stomach begin to affect me almost immediately. My legs begin to twitch; I feel sleepy, "weird," and out of control of my body. In the months to come, I sometimes observe people sleeping through their chemotherapy treatments, apparently seeing it as a welcome opportunity for rest or escape. On this day, I do not easily give up my expectations and/or my desire to stay conscious and aware during the infusion. I regret accepting the "pre-medication" handed me without contemplating their effect. I'm outraged that the drugs have robbed me of alertness; I fight to stay awake and to maintain some semblance of control. It is not to be. Barry gently encourages me to let go of my mental battle and surrender to the way things are since we cannot undo what has occurred. I finally fall into a fitful sleep, trying to stay focused on the affirmations I've worked so hard to create.

I accept this medicine as an ally which will help restore me to optimum health.

I affirm that the sacred medicine I am now receiving will help restore my body to optimum health.

By noon the procedure is almost over. Glad to be awake at last and to have the first infusion behind me, I feel like celebrating in some small way. I have a yen for miso soup. We drive to our favorite Japanese restaurant. It is not yet open for business. We wander into the adjoining gift shop and when we explain my craving and where we have just come from, the cook offers to make some soup for me to take home. In my current state, this seems like an overwhelming kindness.

It is Valentine's Day. Brianna comes to be with me. A decade ago she and I had just survived being robbed and held hostage at gunpoint in her car. Today I've just survived my first chemotherapy treatment for cancer. "Shit happens." "Love heals." We're still here. We're still alive.

My hope of going to Anna's Bat Mitzvah celebration fades as the hours pass and the drugs begin taking over my body. I try to detach and observe this phenomenon but such is the power of the drugs that I feel increasingly sluggish, then weak, then feeble of mind as well as body in the space of a few hours, until I have no strength at all. I simply crawl into bed, inert.

Someone asked me to describe how the chemo affected my body. My first response was that it was indescribable, that I wasn't sure there were words to accurately communicate my experience. How could I possibly describe the insidious weakness that began to overtake me that day after the first infusion? It was as if some huge invisible machine attached itself to my body and began sucking out my energy. I was impotent to stop the process and within hours I felt completely depleted, rendered helpless, robbed of any capacity to move a single muscle, lift my head from the pillow, speak, or even think. It seemed that all I could do was exist.

Soon after, my bowels turned to a muddy mush. When I fell asleep, the mush seemed to ooze through my brain, my nostrils, my eye sockets. It grew and hardened into repulsive shapes stuffing themselves into my mouth as brutish, beastly monsters pummeled and ravaged my body. I was powerless to change or escape from these grotesque and hellish figures, unable to exit from the dreams. I could never have imagined such hideous images. Finally rescued from the horror by waking, my first thought was, "There is no way in hell I am going to go through this process five more times, voluntarily!"

I dreaded sleep lest the nightmares continue, yet I didn't seem able to stay upright or awake for long. Mercifully, the visions were gradually replaced by disjointed, ragged dreams. By the end of the third day, my brain and body adapted or recovered enough to dislodge me from my bed. I even came downstairs, sat on the sofa, and tried to talk. I spoke coherently with friends for awhile, though holding my head upright felt like a huge effort. I awoke the next morning to sweet, sweet blessed relief.

Next to losing one's hair, the thing many people remember most, or sometimes fear most about chemotherapy, is the nausea and the vomiting. Anti-nausea pills are now routinely given to those receiving chemotherapy. After my first chemotherapy infusion I faithfully take the little yellow pills every few hours, even during the night. Taxol is not one of the chemotherapy agents particularly known for causing nausea or stomach upset (a euphemism for vomiting) and Carboplatin is known to cause it. Isaac says that with everything else I'm taking, the little yellow pills are not significant and I should not worry about taking them. I continue to feel, intuitively, that I do not need the Compezine and will eventually decide to try going without it. To my relief, with the exception of a day or two after my last infusion, I experience no nausea. I believe that the acupuncture treatments, the energy healing sessions, and the vitamin B-6 that I take daily may be primarily responsible for my escape from this particular side effect.

Peripheral neuropathy is one of the side effects listed in the informational brochure on Taxol. Like many things one reads about or hears about, the actuality of the experience is quite different from the mental concept. Neuropathy is described as nerve pain, yet pain is something that can usually be isolated and controlled. There is no definition to the irritating, isochronal discomfort in my legs. It feels more like an electric impulse running randomly up and down my legs, causing them to jump and move uncontrollably, making sleep difficult.

As part of my process in deciding whether or not to undergo chemotherapy treatments, I had spoken with a woman who had been diagnosed with the same stage ovarian cancer that I had. She also had the same initial response as me when she was presented with chemotherapy as the medical treatment of choice. She and her family had sought additional opinions and researched the alternatives available before she made the decision to proceed. At the time I spoke with her, she had completed five of the six recommended treatments. In between treatments, she was working with a well-known cancer herbalist and nutritionist whom I had also been in touch with. Her experience and advice was extremely helpful. One thing she emphasized was that her body responded slightly differently to each treatment. She admonished me not to make the mistake of believing that each infusion would affect me the same way or that the experience would get progressively worse. Remembering her words now gives me hope that I might not have to endure the nightmares again. At the same time, I have to face the possibility that the same thing, or something even more challenging, could happen. I must make a conscious decision to go on anyway.

I've been told my hair loss will occur three to four weeks after the first chemotherapy treatment—about the time of the second treatment. I speak with several women who have lost their hair to chemotherapy. One advises me to have my head shaved before the fact. I hear how her family participated in her ritual, her teenage son even videotaping the event. It sounds sane to me. I broach the subject with Meghan, who strenuously objects. She does reluctantly agree to getting my hair cut very short so the transition may not be so startling when my hair does come out. We call a hair stylist friend whom I first met years ago when we were both hospice volunteers. She graciously agrees to come to the house to cut my hair.

For years, I have only allowed my hair to be trimmed, seldom cut. This is drastic, daring, different. It is scary for Meghan and it is exciting for me. The inevitability of the approaching baldness somehow allows me to boldly go where I have not gone before, to let go of that which suddenly seems less necessary.

The short, almost pixie like, haircut has a stunning effect. Meghan loves the haircut! I feel unexpectedly and suddenly liberated! Without a six-inch tumor eating away at my insides, without twenty-five pounds I didn't need, without sugar, without fat, without my long hair, I am freed of so many nonessentials. I am reminded of a native American saying about feeling sorry for oneself, not recognizing that all the while a great wind is carrying one across the sky.

Barry and I are flabbergasted when K. calls after hearing about my cancer and the first thing he says is, "Does Dawn know?" Wow! I guess maybe a cancer diagnosis is still handled that way in some countries or in some families, like when P's father had exploratory surgery and they told her mother his body was full of cancer and they couldn't do anything but sew him back up and she told him that they couldn't find anything. Then everyone had to pretend not to know and as he got weaker and weaker he had to pretend not to know that he knew they knew he really was dying.

I receive letters from a couple of people who have heard of my ovarian cancer diagnosis and who obviously believe my diagnosis is a death sentence. They want to tell me what I have meant to them because they think I am dying! I am touched by their words of praise, flattered even, and yet it is a very strange feeling to be categorized and viewed in this way.

Just when I'm beginning to feel as if I've rejoined the human race, it is time for the next chemotherapy infusion. We go through the same ritual all over again. I pack soda crackers along with the other snacks and bottled water, tapes, pillows, pens, journal, and so on. This time I manage to stay awake during the entire procedure.

The music fills my body like a sweet, warm honey. Little star angels twinkle with light. The star angels are dancing, filling my body with love. The medicine enters and is carried through my body by the honey, which protects me, transforms the medicine by enfolding it in sweetness and lovingly carries it to every part of my body.

An old friend has come from San Diego to see me, bringing music tapes she feels will be therapeutic and healing, and hoping I can go to a gathering of mutual friends with her the next afternoon. I try to explain what happens after my chemotherapy infusion—one good day and then a crash though I wonder how anyone could possibly understand this phenomenon without the benefit of the actual experience. I'm sure I wouldn't have. In the morning I am feeling relatively whole and functional—I even drive my friend to the grocery and buy a few things—and we have an amicable chat. An hour after she leaves I feel the beginning of the insidious energy drain, which slowly increases, until I feel totally and utterly weak.

weak—strong—raw—vulnerable—cry—shake—restless—dream— sleep—wake—defenseless—laugh—cry—love—weak—sleep—rest— drink—dry—thirst—up—down—in—out—strong—weak—heal

I keep a tape recorder by my bedside, and listen to tapes of various teachers from time to time when my mind is alert enough to focus, just taking in the words that resonate and letting the rest go. Some of these tapes have been in my possession for years and they feel like old friends. Others are new gifts from various people. I listen to the old tapes from my changed perspective, with new ears.

Stephen Levine reminds me to cultivate compassion and spaciousness, to make room in my heart for my own suffering. He reminds me to love myself, to forgive myself, to expand my heart to include the effects of the cancer and of the chemotherapy treatments, to have compassion for my own resistance, to let my thoughts and feelings arise and recede without making any one more significant than any other.

Pema Chödrön guides me in a new meditation practice, tonglen, which teaches me how to breathe in suffering as it arises. Whenever something unacceptable, distasteful, or painful presents itself, I breathe it in. I breathe in not just my own suffering but the identical pain of others, of the world. Instead of trying to get rid of the pain, instead of pushing it away, this technique teaches the art of breathing in the hurt, the anger, the chaos, the confusion, or the fear and then breathing out with a sense of spaciousness and calmness.

Jon Kabat-Zinn reminds me that reactivity clouds the mind whereas a thoughtful and imaginative response can create clarity. He reminds me of the power of presence, the importance of patience, and why it is essential to embrace "the full catastrophe."

When my hair is still attached to my head a week after my second chemotherapy treatment, Barry and Meghan begin to believe it may not come out. I know it is inevitable. I just do not know exactly when or how quickly I will become bald. I recall images from television shows where hair clogs the shower drain or a fistful comes out suddenly, leaving a bald spot on the side of the actress' head. From a catalog created by the American Cancer Society specifically for women coping with hair loss from cancer treatment, I order three colored head turbans called "Honeys." I let Meghan pick the colors. I also order a special mesh sleep cap designed to catch hair that may fall out at night to "solve the problem of waking up to find your hair all over the pillow."[4] I never actually use it.

I feel pressured to find a wig before my hair falls out. My best friend offers to go wig shopping with me. She is far more excited about it than I am and tries to convince me it's a perfect opportunity to experiment with a different look. I attempt to enter into the spirit of a new adventure yet it's difficult to muster the energy or to align myself with her enthusiasm. I look for a wig that is the same color and length my hair has been for years. Failing that, I look for something I can live with that doesn't look too fake.

Later in the day, when I bring the two people who care the most about how I will look to the wig shop to give their opinion on which hairpiece to invest in, they cannot agree. We end up going home without a purchase, each of us in our own way emotionally if not physically exhausted by the whole effort and by that which precipitates the necessity of making such a decision.

At the suggestion of an oncology nurse, I sign up for a free "Look Good... Feel Better" seminar put on by the American Cancer Society at a nearby hospital. There are about thirty women in the room, each with some kind and stage of cancer. We are given a "party bag" full of cosmetic products donated by popular companies. There are variations inside the bags. Women begin to strike up conversations and trade products with one another. Casual conversation grows into camaraderie as the inevitable questions are asked and answered.

What kind of cancer do you have? When were you diagnosed? What kind of chemo drugs are you taking? Have you lost your hair yet? Some of the women slowly begin to share their stories, each being careful not to ask too much too soon of any other woman.

A gray-haired lady to my right has leukemia, a result, she has been told, of the chemotherapy she received for some other kind of cancer a dozen years ago. The woman across the table from me is in her twenties. Her parents objected to her marriage and pregnancies at such an early age. Now she has uterine cancer and is thankful she had her three children so young and so close together. She has milky white skin and long, golden hair. It is thick and wavy, surrounding her beautiful face like a halo and flowing halfway down her back. She says she's been told she probably won't lose her hair from her particular kind of chemotherapy. I hope whoever told her so is right.

A woman across the table from me mentions something about her daughter's soccer game and we have a brief dialogue in which we compare our children's ages and leagues. After we apply our make-up, a wig specialist with a sense of humor explains that modern wigs are very well made. He suggests giving one's wig a name and demonstrates how you can throw your wig against a wall or on the floor and even stomp on it if you feel like it, to express yourself on a "bad" day. He says wigs can survive such treatment and that it's very important to let one's anger out.

Photographer: Karl Mondon

In a wig, during a Compassionate Touch® session at Alzheimer's Center

We are told that anyone who wants one will receive a wig today and get it cut and styled, free of charge. Those who do not already have a wig will get first pick. I am amazed that only one other woman besides me raises her hand. I can't believe that most of the women in the room are wearing their wigs. They look so natural! When I arrive in the wig display room, the soccer mom is already there. She has removed her scarf and I notice that her hair is about half gone, leaving large, bald patches on her head. She looks unwell, fragile, and alternately frightened, embarrassed, and angry. My impulse is to say something encouraging or comforting. She looks as if she might cry or yell at any moment. I wonder if she has given herself permission to do either or both when she's alone. I wonder how I look to an unbiased observer. Finally I smile and tell her to choose first because my hair hasn't fallen out yet. Then I move away to give her some privacy.

The wig expert praises my choice of wigs as he adjusts it on my head. He makes a few snips here and there and shows me how to comb and care for the wig. The very cheerful, smiling assistants tell me how great I look.

> And we will wear our turbans and our wigs
> and our scarves
> like banners proclaiming us heroines in the
> struggle.
> We will give up our hair, our vanity, our pride,
> our innocence,
> but we won't give up our hearts, our courage,
> ourselves.

I leave, feeling quite strange wearing make-up and a wig, as if I'm costumed for a play. The woman standing at the door collecting the evaluation cards says brightly, "Do you feel better? You look good!" I dutifully smile and say "yes," and wonder how many of the women here will be alive in two years and why we make how we look matter so much? I fantasize for a moment about a different kind of "Look

Good... Feel Better" event where women would throw off their wigs and maybe their clothing, dance out their stories, kick out their rage, scream out their fears, and cry in each other's arms; an event where everyone would celebrate the indescribable beauty of the authentic self, the beauty that cancer cannot touch or diminish in any way.

One day, crawling into bed with me, Meghan asks if she can see my journal. I show her the one with my drawings and affirmations, not the one with some of my darker narratives. I ask if I can see what she has written in her journal so far and she acquiesces.

Mommy is starting kimo therapy on Thursday or Friday. I am scared, but everything will be alright. Instead of being afraid, I'm trying to be brave. Mommy needs me to be. And about her being bald, I'm trying to make a joke out of it. She might look pretty funny! As hard as it may be, we will get through this. I love my mommy so much.

She has drawn a picture of what she thinks I will look like bald. A few minutes later, she reaches across the bed and touches my hair. "Good-bye hair," she sighs. " I love this hair," she says sweetly. She has bound up all her fears into her anxiety about my hair loss and how I will look bald. "Will it still be you, mommy?" My cancer is forcing her to see herself, and me, in new ways, pushing her to grow stronger, braver, pulling her in different directions. She must adapt, expand, and accept that which seems so unacceptable. Forty-three years apart in age, she and I are faced with the very same task.

When the first of it comes out, I become fascinated with the process of pulling hairs out of my head as I read or talk on the phone. Some come out easily and I examine the roots before dropping them in the trash. Some hair sticks stubbornly to my head, refusing to budge until days later. A few bits at the nape of my neck seem to actually grow longer and are light and soft. Barry calls them my "wise hairs" and it is weeks before they disappear.

Walking past a mirror today, my facade of not caring about losing my hair suddenly collapses. What I truly believed was a non-issue for me suddenly becomes an issue now that it is actually happening… I'm offered a symbol of liberation, of transformation, and yet I whine, cry, and complain. "But I look so different!" my mind screams. And when I put on the wig I look like someone else. What will people think? Must I lose my eyebrows too, maybe even my eyelashes? Must I be completely stripped?

As we snuggle in my bed reading together, Meghan studies my face and suddenly exclaims, "Mommy, your eyelashes are gone!" I wasn't sure when she'd notice. It isn't completely true—three or four lashes still cling tenaciously to my eyelids. Before the month is out, they are gone, as is every other hair on my body, as far as I can tell.

My eyelashes are gone. I can't give Meghan butterfly kisses. I know my eyelashes will grow back. I know there are a hundred worse things but right now I just miss my eyelashes. Surely losing all the hair on one's body is a small price to pay for life! My hair is dying but I am alive. My skin is dying but I am alive. The cancer cells are dying, but I am alive!

I commit myself to full health. I vow to respect and revere my body, to eat only foods that will nourish and heal my body. To breathe, to move, to love, to play, to live!

The third chemotherapy infusion brings the now familiar pattern of a day and a half of feeling relatively "good" followed by the "zap" to my energy and subsequent weakening. This time, however, the meltdown seems to be more mental and emotional than it is physical.

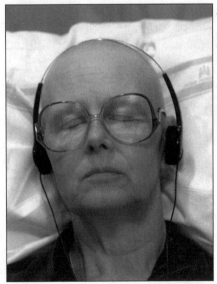

Photographer: Karl Mondon

Listening to music tape during chemotherapy infusion

Sleep escapes me. I don't seem to feel any different lying down than staying up so I continue walking around, doing whatever there is to do. Nothing seems real. It seems as if there is nothing stable to grab hold of, nothing is known, nothing predictable. This, in itself, is not unlike what has occurred for me during intensive meditation retreats. In both cases, there is nothing to do but surrender to the way it is. I do not have enough energy to pretend that things are different than they are, or to distract myself.

I feel totally out of control in every conceivable way. I want strawberry shortcake, apple pie, french-fries—anything that is not macrobiotic! I am on an emotional roller coaster that seems to have no exit platform. My fingers are tingling, my heart palpitating. Thoughts rise and fall away, tears come in like an ocean wave and recede just as quickly. I feel raw, exposed, vulnerable, fragile and utterly defenseless. I'm too hot, then too cold, boundless, confined, overwhelmed, confused, all alone in a crowd and even with the ones I love the most.

A few days before my chemotherapy sessions, and about a week afterwards, Isaac works on my physical body—taking my pulses, examining my tongue, looking at my latest blood tests, asking questions, and making adjustments in both where he inserts the needles during my treatment and the herb formula I will take home—and Nancy works on my ethereal body. I fully believe that the unique skills of these two people are instrumental in helping me tolerate the toxic effects of the chemotherapy and in giving me additional support for recovery. As difficult as it is, it could be far worse without their help.

Sometimes it feels as if I am sleepwalking through my days. My body performs all the necessary functions, yet a mist-like grayness pervades my being. I feel trapped in a kind of half-life existence. The star angels who guide the chemo drugs seem to be sleeping. I need new images, something to strengthen my immune system, increase the white cells.

Stephan comes and uses the tuning forks on my body. When I try to visualize the white cells, I see only a few, all clustered on the left side of my upper abdomen. I ask them for help in making my body stronger.

A small setback occurs after my fourth chemotherapy infusion. My neutrophils (blood cells produced in the bone marrow) are not coming back quickly enough after their recent demise. This condition is, we are told, a common occurrence during chemotherapy treatment, yet the fact that my body was unable to do something this time that it did successfully three other times, makes me feel that I have somehow failed. The doctor wants to postpone the next treatment which means my completion date will be pushed back. My carefully planned schedule is thrown off; my expectations of when I will reach the finish line of this particular marathon are dashed. My mind rebels and I plummet into a deep, albeit temporary, depression.

Sometimes I want so much to just forget I have cancer. I want to pretend that life is not precarious. I want to eat whatever looks good to me in the moment. I want to do whatever I feel like doing! I want my habits, my hair, my life, my innocence back! I want off the roller coaster!

We are told that the "cure" for neutropenia is a series of neupogen (a product of recombinant-DNA technology) injections to stimulate quicker growth of the neutrophils. The side effects of these injections include bone pain and flu-like symptoms such as aching all over. Oddly enough, the extra needle sticks concern me more than the side effects. I am given a list of things to avoid—crowds and unnecessary exposure to the public, sick people, uncooked vegetables and fresh fruits, ice—and things to watch for such as bleeding from gums, urine, nose, stool, skin, or "other." One of the oncology nurses says to rest a lot and eat well and maybe if my count goes up enough I can still stay on schedule.

I wonder if I "blew" it by teaching for three days or by speaking at the conference and I resolve to get more rest this month. I call Isaac, who says he can boost the white count with herbs but then I develop a case of herpes, which apparently renders the herbs less effective.

Teaching 3-day workshop between second and third chemotherapy treatments

When I attempt to visualize the white cells inside my body multiplying, I see little molecule like circles with happy (smiley) faces. They say, "We'll come to the party! We'll help you! All you have to do is invite us!" I see a string of white Christmas lights surrounding my body on an energetic level, providing light and a party atmosphere. The smiley-faced white cells begin multiplying and expanding and they eventually fill my whole body.

I continue my affirmations— singing the words in a variety of configurations and setting them to tunes conjured up from my childhood. I make four trips to the hospital this week, three for the injections and one for new blood tests.

I am happy, I am healthy, I am strong!

I choose health, I choose life, I choose joy!

When I become discouraged I think of the hospice patients and nursing home residents I have known and of the incredible physical challenges some of them withstood while living with various diseases which ultimately took their lives. I think of all that Fran endured after her multiple surgeries, radiation, and chemotherapy treatments during the two years of our relationship—the endless leg spasms and pain, constipation, diarrhea, nausea, infected pressure sores, eventual paralysis of both legs, and bouts of depression. I think of the 45 pills a day she took to manage various conditions caused by her disease process and to counteract symptoms caused by the other medications. I hear her voice as she speaks of taking one day at a time, of how much she has to be grateful for, and of how the cancer has taught her patience.

I think of the young computer genius with non-Hodgkin's Lymphoma, of the valiant effort he made to keep working at home so he could keep his job, and how he used his last bit of strength to go on a cruise with his wife the month before he died. I think of the brilliant musician, just weeks before his death from AIDS, throwing a holiday party for his suburban neighbors and making sure there were plenty of candy-filled stockings to hand out to the children.

I think of Bob, living for fifteen years with a rare neuromuscular disease that caused continuous spasms in his shoulder, neck, and face. In the eight months I knew him, he was bedridden, hooked up to a feeding tube and a catheter, unable to speak clearly or to swallow well. In spite of his increasing physical limitations and his almost constant pain, I never once heard him, or his wife, who had shouldered the heavy burden of caregiving, complain about anything. They both retained a pleasant, cheerful countenance, a sense of humor, and even an ability to continue helping others less fortunate than themselves.

I think of the young woman living out her days in an extended care hospital, rendered helpless by a motorcycle accident, of the middle-aged doctor felled by a stroke, and the sweet-looking grandmother who no longer recognizes anyone in her family or remembers her own name. I think of Christopher Reeve, and less famous individuals in similar circumstances, who have transcended unexpected and unthinkable traumas and heartache to achieve a state of wholeness and health that many people in perfect physical condition have not achieved.

I think of my cousin whose nine-year-old daughter has had leukemia since she was six—with chemotherapy, radiation, remission, recurrence, and numerous complications. And I immediately feel lucky. I am the one who has cancer, not one of my children.

An older woman standing next to me picking out vegetables at the store, points to my head and says with a twinkle in her eye, "Do you have what I have under there?" pulling up her wig just enough to reveal her baldness. Without waiting for an answer, she smiles and scurries away. Can she spot a wig that easily? Do I look like I have cancer? Maybe I have "chemotherapy glow?"

We are the first to arrive in the infusion room. "Your chair is waiting," one of the nurses says, smiling, as we enter the large room. We move directly to "our" spot in the far corner near the windows, where we have a clear view of the nurse's station as well as the half dozen other infusion units, and settle in. In a short time and unlike

With Barry during a chemotherapy infusion

other days when we've been alone, at least for the first hour or so, the room begins to fill to its capacity. A middle-aged man who has come alone takes the chair in the corner across from us. As soon as he is "hooked up" he pushes his chair back, puts on the headphones provided, and turns on his television set. An older lady with a cane, her son in attendance, chooses another corner chair. Her son opens a book and once her infusion begins, she falls asleep. An attractive four-person family occupies another space—the patient, her husband, and their two young adult children. They talk animatedly among themselves planning details of the daughter's upcoming wedding. They all leave a short time later, the mother wearing a small bag under her blouse, attached to a shunt. Her husband is given instructions for flushing the bag. The gray-haired "pink lady" is here offering juice and blankets. A middle-aged man arrives, accompanied by his wife. They are obviously familiar with the routine. The friendly blond nurse moves efficiently around the room, passing out smiles and jokes, affectionately calling us everything from "sweet pea" to "baby doll." We have come together in a crucible of parallel universes—the people who have cancer, the people who love the people who have cancer, and the people trying to help cure the people who have cancer.

Today my star angels are bowing down in gassho to the pre-medications and to the chemotherapy drugs as they enter my body!

Halfway through the morning, I discover I have made a tactical error. I have worn a one-piece jump suit instead of my usual pants and top. Going to the bathroom while hooked up to an IV isn't usually that big a problem, as long as there is someone to push the IV stand, help with the necessary partial removal of clothing, and stand by while the deed is done. Removing a one-piece zip-up garment while hooked up to an IV stand is a bit trickier! Not wanting to interrupt the infusion and delay our departure, we use ingenuity, patience, and persistence in solving the puzzle. The whole procedure, had it been videotaped, would have given everyone a good laugh.

The day after this infusion, I find myself waiting to go down for the count and instead a small miracle occurs. The knockout never happens! This particular treatment will live forever in my memory, not because of its difficulties but because it is almost a non-event—a little dip in energy, instead of a nose-dive off a cliff! In spite of this,

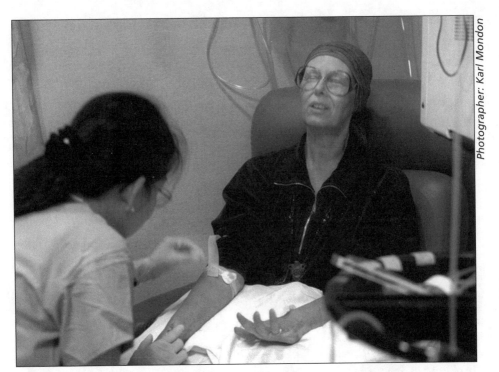

Reacting to needle being inserted into vein for a chemotherapy infusion

neupogen injections are again required to build up my white count before the next infusion, which will then kill all the white cells once more. I have the realization that the same thing is quite likely to occur after the last infusion and that the shots will continue even then.

*I barely make it to my car in the parking lot before I burst into tears. Why? Because I'm so tired of being stuck with needles! I hate these daily shots. I hate these endless blood tests! How do diabetics give themselves shots day after day? How do people **do** this?!*

The oncology nurses in the infusion room are upbeat and congratulatory whenever someone comes in for the last of his or her prescribed chemotherapy treatments. Today is my graduation day. In the mood of getting it over with, the drip is speeded up—I never even realized this was an option—and we are in and out in just over three hours as opposed to four. There are pictures taken and hugs all around. The elation my husband expresses in this moment seems much greater than my own. I still have to get through the next week and I also know that what happens next is entirely unpredictable. I try to steady my mind, keep it in neutral at least, without expectations or fantasies.

After one day of quiet celebration interspersed with fluctuating and conflicting emotions, my "down" period begins. It turns out to be quite distinct from the others, and one of the more challenging of the six infusions. A new after-effect is dry mouth. No matter how much I drink, the inside of my mouth feels like cotton. Bleah! I experience the familiar fatigue with the added twist of feeling on the edge of nausea and having no appetite. Still another new effect is heart palpitations. I am convinced the fast drip is partially responsible for these new effects though it is impossible to know. The following week my white count is still very low.

Why do I feel like I have done something wrong, failed in some way every time my white count plummets and I need the shots again? Why do I hate needles so much? Why do I fantasize that the neupogen shots might not work this time around?

Next on the oncologist's agenda is a CT scan to check for any sign of cancer in my body at this point. He comes up with a brilliant plan to minimize my anxiety about the procedure. He suggests I go to the infusion unit first and have one of the nurses there do the needle stick instead of a doctor in the x-ray unit. This works well and cuts time off the whole procedure.

Since the CA-125 blood test has registered under 5 every time its been taken since my surgery, my oncologists suspect that it may be a marker for me after all. They think that what is normal for most people may have simply been high for me. Hopefully their theory will never be tested.

Buoyed by the "squeaky-clean" CT scan results presented by the doctor today, Barry says to Meghan, "Do you realize what this means, sweetie? There is no cancer in mommy's body." Her face expands in a look of surprise and hope as she says incredulously, "That's it? It's over?" "Well of course it **could come back** *but it is gone for now, and hopefully forever." Her brief moment of joy is snatched away by the only three words she hears.*

Certainly there are diseases far more catastrophic in their nature than cancer; several of them listed before one even reaches the big "C" in the alphabet! A diagnosis of AIDS, Alzheimer's, or ALS would be more devastating to most people than almost any form of cancer, and I imagine nearly everyone would chose cancer over life as a quadriplegic. The thing is we don't get to choose. Maybe we get what we most need, maybe we have made some contract on a soul level before our birth, maybe we intersect with our karmic destiny; most likely it's a combination of genetics, pollution, stress, and diet and maybe its just plan bad luck. Each and every one of us will die of something. Maybe the more important point is not what we die of but how we die, and even more important, how well we live until we die.

There is a story in the Old Testament, which is often referred to as *Jacob Wrestling with the Angel*, although the word angel is not actually mentioned anywhere in the passage. During a stressful period in his life, Jacob leaves his home in Haran to move back to Canaan, which he had left twenty years before. As this long and arduous journey is nearing an end, he decides one day to send his family, the servants, and all of his belongings on ahead of him across a stream. There is no clue in the story as to why he did this. Perhaps he just wants some "down time" away from his large entourage, which includes eleven children, two wives, and two handmaidens. Perhaps he is seeking a quiet space for personal contemplation. In any case, he spends that night by himself, alongside a stream.

"And Jacob was left alone; and a man wrestled with him until the breaking of the day. And when he saw that he prevailed not against him, he touched the hollow of his thigh; and Jacob's thigh was put out of joint as he wrestled with him."[5] As daylight approaches, the mysterious opponent asks Jacob to let him go but Jacob refuses, saying, "I will not let you go, unless you bless me."[6]

This other being just shows up in Jacob's space in the dark of night, uninvited, unbidden, and engages him in combat. Now Jacob doesn't whine, "Why me?" or "Why now?" or complain, "Hey, I don't deserve this." He doesn't try to run away. He doesn't shout, "You're just an illusion. I'm going to pretend you're not here." He accepts the reality of the situation and he wrestles with the intruder. He throws himself into the encounter, becoming fully engaged. Even when he is hurt, he doesn't give up; he keeps going, in the dark, through the entire night. He stays with it and he does not succumb. Then, as darkness fades and the light of morning once again appears, his opponent wants to concede, but Jacob demands that the aggressor bless him before he will let him go! Jacob insists on something more than residual pain from his ordeal. He is not willing to settle for release or comfort or safety. He wants meaning, understanding. He is looking for Grace after a gritty night of combat! And so his unusual nighttime visitor complies with his request. He gives Jacob a new name, a new identity that symbolizes a transformation, and opens a whole new way of life for this man now called Israel.

The blessing Jacob receives is probably not obvious to other people right away—they only notice he is limping—yet Jacob knows that he is a changed man. Before he leaves the place where this life-altering event has occurred, Jacob gives it a name that, in Hebrew means, "I have come face to face with God."

My daily life now does not look very different than it did before my cancer diagnosis and treatment. I do most of the same things I used to do—cheer my youngest daughter on at her soccer and softball games, clean the house, do the laundry, teach workshops, write, speak at conferences, socialize with friends. And, while my physical appearance has been changed by cancer to the degree that some old friends do not easily recognize me, other than an inexplicable new predilection for wearing red shoes, my personality is much the same as it was before I had cancer. I am still easily distracted. I struggle over simple decisions, I cry at sappy movies, I make judgements, I get irritable when the house is messy, I forget the punch lines of jokes when I try to repeat them, and I continually over-estimate how much I can get done in a day. My inner experience, however, is irrevocably and dramatically changed. I consider the unexpected challenge of cancer a true blessing because it has transformed my life. I am a new person, a different person, a better person.

Chapter Seven

Cancer's Lessons, Cancer's Gifts

*It's only when we truly know and understand
that we have a limited time on earth—and
that we have no way of knowing when our
time is up—that we will begin to live each
day to the fullest, as if it was the only one we
had.*

Elisabeth Kubler-Ross

Helen Keller once stated that life is a succession of lessons which must be lived to be understood. When life handed me a cancer diagnosis, I made a choice to open to the experience of that cancer and to learn from whatever occurred instead of just trying to "get through" it somehow or to pray for recovery. In deciding to make friends with my disease and in accepting the cancer as a teacher, I determined to get as much as I could from the curriculum. This particular course in living required my full attention for about a year, and my education is ongoing. Some of the lessons have been obvious and some have been harder to discern and integrate. They are still unfolding and deepening. Some of the lessons I might have eventually gleaned in some other way. Others perhaps could only have come to me through something as dramatic and traumatic as a life-threatening illness.

Cancer has taught me to pay attention, almost as if I have been awakened from a deep and habitual sleep and am finally present. I am more conscious of my actions and my reactions. I notice with increased frequency, how reactivity clouds the mind and dissipates energy whereas responding tends to evoke clarity and promote vitality. I spend less time than I used to criticizing, dramatizing, and agonizing. I notice that fear and guilt—though not totally vanquished—have much less control over my mind.

I act less, now, out of habit. I do not sacrifice my own needs for others out of a neurotic desire to please, pacify, or avoid conflict. I put myself in the equation of the balancing act of human relationships. I rest when I am tired. I take better care of my body. I take more pleasure in the innumerable miracles of everyday life as I breathe it in. I remember to breathe out. I find it easier to forgive others, and myself. My ability to give and receive love has increased. My sense of what is possible has expanded. I complain less, I don't procrastinate as much as I used to, and I no longer take anything for granted!

Part of almost any cancer diagnosis is the elemental lesson of the realization that life is short at best, and that we are not immortal. Though impermanence is the basic nature of life, we often forget this inherent truth until some significant loss or threat to our existence jogs our memory.

Cancer has drawn my attention to the immediacy of life to the degree that distraction and procrastination have become less habitual for me. I have less trouble staying on purpose and completing tasks than I used to. If there is something I really want to do, I usually do it. I make a greater effort to keep my communications current. I do not leave things I want to say unsaid. I clear up misunderstandings as soon as possible. I am quicker to apologize when I recognize I may have said or done something thoughtless or hurtful to another.

I believe it was Gay Luce who once said that we spend more time making preparations for the next vacation we hope to take than we do preparing for the irrefutable event of our own death. We are, by and large, a death denying society. Most people do not set aside time to think about or talk about their own death, nor does the general population want to hear the details about someone else's death. At social gatherings or when one is being introduced to new people, the question, "What do you do?" usually arises at some point. During the years when I was spending a lot of time with hospice patients and with the frail elderly in nursing homes, I would usually answer that I worked with the dying. I found that not many people wanted to hear about that. They would often mumble something like "oh, good for you" or "how depressing" and quickly excuse themselves.

Receiving a diagnosis of a life-threatening disease—one that I have watched people die from—has given me an opportunity to prepare for my death, not in a morbid, depressing way but in a facing reality kind of way. It has given me the opportunity to contemplate what I have accomplished in life which, to my surprise, really turns out to be a great deal. It has given me the chance to consider what I really want to do with the rest of my life—whether I live another five months, five years, or fifty years—to reflect on changes I can make, on patterns of behavior I can choose to let go of, and others which I want to bring into being.

After a cancer diagnosis, you may have to keep paying the bills and doing the laundry, as one survivor put it, but "you live your life by a shorter list." Cancer has taught me to focus more on what really matters and let the rest go, not to "sweat the small stuff" as the popular book title proclaims. I spend more time doing the things I truly want to do, and being with the people I truly want to be with. I try to spend time with people who are happy, positive, and enjoying life and avoid those who constantly complain about how bad things are. I engage in activities that lighten my heart, promote creativity, and nourish my spirit.

Looking back on the fact that the world didn't stop when my mail went unanswered, when I didn't return phone calls right away, when my closets remained unorganized, or when photographs weren't immediately put into albums, I realize how much of my behavior in life has come from habitual and unconscious patterns, from preconceived ideas about wanting to please or impress others. Cancer has given me the opportunity to let go of trying to live up to impossible self-imposed standards. I am relieved of the guilt, anxiety, and stress which that behavior created. I am living a more creative and a more authentic life. I am certain that I am loved for who I am not for how I look or for how my house looks.

My husband says that life requires our attendance. Cancer has roused me from inertia, and has summoned my presence. I am no longer content to stand on the shore and watch the scenery. Cancer stripped me bare, threw me naked into the middle of life's ocean and soaked me to the bone. As I dry myself off, I am a different person, and I will never be the same again. I have begun to experience the myriad textures, colors, and forms of life in a richer, fuller way. I laugh more. I am less afraid. I don't mean that I have suddenly developed a passion for sky-diving or river-rafting (though I am certainly more open to the idea of taking part in such activities than I once was). I mean that I am in the picture instead of looking at the picture. The glass wall between my life and me has been shattered. Cancer has taught me to own my life and to celebrate it.

Cancer has brought me back into a more conscious relationship with my physical body. Not only had I taken my body for granted for most of my adult life, but I had also neglected to take good care of it for at least a decade. I had never lost extra weight gained after pregnancy and childbirth at age forty-three, and regular exercise was something I thought I did not have time for. Although I ate what would probably be considered a "good" diet, I consumed more food than I needed, often ate hurriedly, "on the run," or while engaged in other activities such as reading or fervent conversations. In addition,

I remained addicted to sweets, convincing myself that if something contained honey or fructose instead of sugar, it was "okay" to eat all I wanted of it.

Years ago I took, and later taught, various movement, body awareness, and relaxation classes, practiced yoga, and for a couple of years, ran on a daily basis. As a massage therapist I have touched hundreds of bodies and supported others in "tuning in." Yet, somehow, before cancer became a personal experience, a particular conscious awareness of the nuances of my own physical body and its functions had eluded me.

My illness has startled me into paying much more attention to my physical body. I have become ultra sensitive to and aware of any changes that occur. I have begun to recognize the significance of my body and of my relationship to it. I have begun to heal that relationship.

Cancer has given me a new and true awareness of the symbiotic connection between my physical body and me. I have come to understand, on a deeper level than ever before, the reality of my body as a shelter for the spirit, and as a vehicle for my awakening. This realization has given rise to a new awareness in me of the sacred responsibility I have to honor my body, to respect it, and to treat it with care.

The most exciting thing is happening. I feel sometimes almost as if I am discovering my body for the first time. I have tiny glimpses of what it is like for those who have never forgotten the purpose of their bodies or for athletes who are finely attuned to every subtlety of physical functioning.

I am aware of the working of joints, muscles, and tendons in my own body in a way that I have never experientially understood before, even during my study of anatomy and physiology training years ago. I am more conscious of my body movements, of the relationship that each part of my body has to each other part, and of the relationship of my body to the earth that supports it.

I inhabit my body differently. I treat my body differently. I listen to my body and the messages it sends me. I have developed an appreciation for my body's cellular wisdom. I value my body in a way that I have not before.

When I stand naked in front of a mirror, I no longer see wrinkles, scars, sagging skin, flaws, and imperfections. I no longer see a body I wish looked better or different. I see something amazing in its functionality, beautiful in its form, a miraculous framework that carries, contains, and supports me! I am so much more than my body and yet this body I see and touch is a very important part of me. I love the body I've been given, perhaps for the first time in my entire relationship with it.

Cancer has transformed my relationship to food. My decision to eat differently, to pay closer attention to what I put into my body, has increased my understanding of how my body uses food to give me energy. As I practice new eating habits—preparing food more simply, chewing slowly and mindfully—the activity has become a more conscious, meaningful, and pleasurable experience. Meals and even snacks have become sacred healing rituals.

I remember vividly an occasion, before I had cancer, when I threw a tea bag into a cup and poured boiling water over it. Some time later I reach out for the cup only to find it empty! "How could that be?" I thought. "I was so looking forward to drinking my tea! My mind must be playing tricks on me." I check the teapot. It is still warm. I check the teabag. It is still wet. I finally realize that, distracted by mental preoccupations and multiple tasking, I have drunk the tea without even realizing it. This experience startles and shocks me. How many cups of tea might I have downed in such an unconscious state? How many times, I wonder, do we keep eating and drinking more in search of the actual experience?

Thich Nhat Hanh tells a wonderful story in his book *Living Buddha, Living Christ* in which someone asks the Buddha what he and his monks practice. The Buddha replies "We sit, we walk, and we eat." When the questioner protests that everyone sits, walks, and eats, the Buddha responds, "But when we sit we know we are sitting, when we walk we know we are walking, and when we eat we know we are eating."[7]

Having cancer has taught me the exquisite grace of doing one thing at a time. Now—not always, yet often—when I make a cup of tea, I notice the shape and color of the cup I choose as the container for my tea, I hear the sound of the water filling the cup, I feel the warmth on my hands as I hold the cup. Inhaling the aroma, savoring the taste, I experience the sensation of the tea passing through my lips onto my tongue and sliding down my throat. I am thankful that I am alive and able to enjoy this particular experience in this particular moment, which will never come again. I am thankful I can sit in peaceful silence, that I can move my hands to raise the cup to my lips, and that I can smell, taste, and swallow. Drinking my cup of tea thus becomes a conscious, nourishing, satisfying, and healing event.

Sitting in the café section at the bookstore, I smell blueberry muffins baking. The unique scent wafts across the space and settles in my nostrils. The aroma is heady, intoxicating, mouth watering. For a brief moment I consider leaving so I won't be tempted to buy and eat one of the muffins. Then, instead of shutting it out, I decide to take the scent in. I close my eyes. I inhale deeply and allow myself to totally enjoy the sweet smell of the muffins baking and all the pleasurable memories and images the smell evokes. I feel nourished by the aroma and not at all deprived because I'm not eating the muffin! The smell itself is delicious and satisfying—an unexpected gift. I feel incredibly grateful that I am alive, that I can smell and breathe. I cherish this moment.

The muffin experience recorded in my journal would not have occurred before I had cancer. In the same situation, I would have used my will to reinforce my decision not to eat something I thought would be unhealthy. I would have flip-flopped between feeling smug and bereft, and eventually would have rationalized my way into eating the muffin or whatever else it might have been that I thought I shouldn't have, yet desired.

This particular mental construct no longer has power in my mind, not because I am afraid my cancer will return and kill me if I eat a little sugar or fat, but because I have made a conscious decision and a commitment to eat only that which I feel will best serve my body in healing, recovery, and future health. Apparently, it took being diagnosed with an aggressive, life-threatening disease to bring me to such a commitment.

Cancer has taught me to cultivate gratitude, which has contributed to my experience of abundance. Gratitude may be born at the sound of your child's first cry, watching a magnificent sunset, or receiving the results of a negative biopsy. It may emerge in an oncology infusion room when the needle goes in on the first try or in the moment you regain the ability to turn onto your side in sleep and recover the immeasurable comfort of your loved one's back. Gratitude allows us to experience our wholeness, no matter what the condition of our physical bodies may be. Gratitude opens our hearts and our minds. Gratitude amplifies our capacity to receive.

I have learned that gratitude is also an infallible cure for self-pity or the "doldrums," for reversing irritability, and for creating the experience of abundance. Whenever I remember to look at a cup as half full instead of half empty, that cup is soon overflowing.

I was recently feeling overwhelmed and irritable, wishing certain family members would comply with my agenda and help out more with cleaning, shopping, decorating for the holidays, and so on. My state of upset was escalating rather quickly and I realized that if I kept feeding the thoughts I was having, I would probably bite the head off the next person to walk through the front door! I began to sing my old mantra "one step at a time," recognizing that I was missing the preciousness of the present moment. I happened to be vacuuming at the time. When I put my attention on just that, what I noticed was a sense of gratitude. I experienced gratitude for the beautiful floor covering, for the luxury of the sophisticated equipment that was making my task so much easier than it might have been, for electricity, for my ability to bend over, for the physical stamina which allowed me to clean the house, and so on. My grumpy mood soon disappeared and I experienced a new surge of creative energy.

I often use the time spent driving to and from appointments, when I am alone in my car, as an opportunity to create a thankful list. I say or sing aloud the things that arise in my mind, in the moment, for which I am grateful. The day came when I heard myself say, "I am thankful for my cancer." My logical mind reacted in shock; surely being thankful for cancer makes no sense! Pausing to examine the notion, I realized that my spontaneous admission was authentic. I *am* truly thankful for my encounter with cancer, for all that it is teaching me, and for the changes that have occurred in my life as a result of this experience. I have come to agree with the woman who took the microphone at a Stephen Levine workshop to announce that she had been graced with cancer. She went on to explain that it wasn't until she got cancer that she started to pay attention to the preciousness of each breath, to the momentum of each thought, and to begin to directly experience her life. There truly are many paths to the present moment.

Navaho Indian parents traditionally take even their youngest children outdoors each morning to greet the day. They teach their children that each sunrise is a Gift and that the day must be used wisely in order to honor the Giver.

Cancer has taught me to welcome the morning differently, to pause and experience the wondrous grace of a new day, as if each dawn is a kiss from God. Now, before getting out of bed each morning, I take a few minutes to make a mental note of one hundred things I am thankful for. Sometimes I make an alphabetical list, sometimes I just let the list unfold stream of consciousness style, sometimes I go by category. It is not the end of my gratitude practice. It just feels like a good way to start the day.

As I get out of bed, I make a conscious choice to embrace the day, whatever it may bring. I honor the new day in some small way— lighting a candle, reading an inspirational poem, or repeating a prayer or an affirmation. I embrace my body, recognizing my relationship to my body and my body's relationship to the earth. I breathe deeply. I ask for guidance in making thoughtful decisions, in making this day count, and in remembering not to waste the precious time I have been given. As I lay down to sleep at the end of the day, I recall the gifts and the lessons the day has brought, remembering to give thanks for the blessing of the day itself.

My experience with cancer has taught me to take no thing for granted. It has given me the experience that whatever discomfort I may be experiencing, whatever challenges a day or an hour may hold, those things are not as important or as significant as my aliveness, as the unwavering sweetness of life itself. I have begun to grasp the sacredness of being.

Cancer does not happen to an individual. It happens to a family and its effects extend to everyone who has a connection or an attachment to the person who receives the diagnosis. When my budding adolescent tells me how happy she is that I don't have cancer any more, a part of my mind wonders if that is an irrefutable fact. Then I ask her, "What was the hardest part for you?"

"You losing your hair, you going to the hospital and seeing you like that and fainting and just realizing that you had cancer which I thought would never happen and I never even thought about it and now I think about it all the time." As my tears fall over her shattered innocence, I sense strength and courage building in its place.

She continues, "Seeing you getting all that chemo, I never ever thought that would happen to anyone in my family and now I know that it is possible and it scares me. If one of us had gotten badly hurt in a car crash I would probably think about that all the time and then that would scare me."

I inquire of this loquacious child what she has learned from me having cancer and she answers thoughtfully, "If you believe and if you don't give up, then you can cope with it. I guess it taught me that, and if I ever get cancer, that if I believe in myself, as scary as it is, it will be okay probably and if you take care of yourself which you were really good at... " her voice trails off and there are no more words because she is in my arms and we are both crying. We have each made it to this moment. We are both still learning how to live. We are both learning that being brave doesn't mean not being afraid, it means going on anyway when you are scared.

Lance Armstrong, a 27-year old American cyclist won the Tour de France, a grueling 21-day race in 1999, less than three years after undergoing surgery, chemotherapy and radiation for metastasized testicular cancer — he had been given less than a 40% chance of surviving. In an interview with Barbara Walters, Lance said that winning the Tour de France was a great experience but "all things being equal I'd take the cancer." In another television interview after securing the coveted first place trophy for the second time in 2000, he called cancer the most important event of his life and said he'd rather be remembered as a cancer survivor than as a two-time winner of the Tour de France.

The turn of the century this year has given rise to much reflection in regard to prioritizing and remembering momentous events, significant incidents, important inventions, changes, and so on. In contemplating the most consequential events in my own life in the past century, having cancer is certainly among the top qualifiers. It is a trenchant reminder of a turning point in my life, the gateway to a new way of being and seeing and loving.

Cancer has unveiled the eyes of my heart. It has enabled me to behold beauty that I did not see before. It has uncovered for me a vibrant, rich layer of life I did not know existed. It has allowed me to access a deeper joy in being alive than I was able to before. Cancer has propelled me into the center of life. It has given me entry into a hallowed inner sanctum of reality that allows me to experience the abundance, radiance, peace, and harmony that is always accessible, even in the midst of chaos and confusion.

Whatever the future holds for me, cancer has taught me that I can say yes to life, I can allow my passion, my awe, my grief, my joy, to emerge and to express itself. In the midst of chaos and catastrophe, devastation, disaster, and all the dualities of existence, I can still open to, and embrace my life.

Cancer has opened my spirit to the infinite grace and beauty and fluidity of life. It has given me new reverence for my own breathing out and breathing in, inside the day's sacred rhythms. It has contributed to my sense of awe in experiencing my aliveness within the magnificence, mystery, and majesty of creation, which is sometimes so achingly beautiful that I must stretch my soul to take it in. The words of Emily, the young heroine in Thornton Wilder's *Our Town,* resonate with me in a way they couldn't when I was reciting them on stage as a high-school senior, "Oh earth, you're too wonderful for anybody to realize you!"[8]

Cancer has accentuated for me the unpredictability of our sojourn on earth; it has heightened my awareness of both the fragility and the strength of life. Cancer has left me with a searing reminder of the impermanence of all things. The vicissitudes of life are myriad. Change is constant. Fortunes are made and lost. Houses are built and burn to the ground, are rebuilt, and sometimes burn again. Natural disasters kill hundreds of thousands of people in the space of a few minutes. Loved ones die suddenly, a lifetime of quadriplegia begins in a split second of inattentiveness or miscalculation, the unthinkable occurs.

Stephen Levine tells a shocking and mesmerizing story about a young couple who shared a love of hiking and taking nature photos.

This couple had a dream to climb a particular mountain they had only seen in pictures. They saved their money for many years and on their 10th wedding anniversary, traveled to the country to climb the mountain. As they hiked higher and higher, they finally came upon the magnificent waterfall they had waited so long to see. The sound of the water rushing over the cliffs was deafening. As they paused on the trail to take in the beauty that was at last theirs to behold, the wife stepped back to take a picture. A few moments later, her husband turned around, the joy of the shared moment alive on his face, and his wife was not there. She had disappeared, fallen to her death, her screams no doubt unheard over the roar of the waterfall.

All we ever truly have is the present moment. What we make of our moments is up to us. We do not have to travel to exotic places, climb high mountains, walk in a labyrinth, bathe in special waters, or seek out a vortex to experience the sacred. We do not need to be inside a temple, cathedral, or sweat lodge to experience spirit. We resonate with the energy, experience the beauty, or feel calmed in such places because our senses are alerted, our attention is stabilized, and our hearts and minds are open; and because we are experiencing the power of many others before us who have been similarly focused in that particular space.

By paying attention, by letting go of our desire for things to be one way or another way, and by opening to the way things actually are, we can, at any time, enter the sacred realm. It is our recognition of the divine in others and in ourselves that makes the ground upon which we stand hallowed. It is our unconditional and unpreferenced presence in the moment that makes it holy and makes us whole.

There is no situation, no relationship, no event in life that does not hold the potential for healing. There is no moment that is not an opportunity for awakening.

Chapter Eight

Life Goes On

Don't worry, life goes on.

Dr. Edward Barankin

The oncologist explains that the tumors in the lung are growing and that, medically speaking, there is nothing further to recommend. He offers to refer my father-in-law to hospice. Thinking hospice is a place where people go to die, my husband assures the doctor that we will care for his father in our home if and when it becomes necessary. The oncologist asks Ed if he wants heroic measures taken should hospitalization become necessary. Ed answers clearly and with little hesitation that he does not want heroic measures taken. He is then asked to sign a paper to this effect. I hear my husband's heart crying as he digests his father's decision, and accepts the finality of it, modeling his own behavior on this man he respects more than any other.

As we leave the doctor's office, I linger behind a moment. "His face seems a little jaundiced," I say. "Yes," the doctor replies, giving me information that was not mentioned at any time during the just completed visit. "I'm sure the cancer is in his liver. In fact, I imagine it's all over his body now."

A week or two later, Ed calls early on a Saturday morning asking if we can come to his apartment. Since his cancer diagnosis, my husband has spent a good deal of time with his father, participating in his care after surgery to remove a third of his lung, accompanying him to appointments, taking him for long drives. Their already close relationship has become more physical and much more intimate. Ed's malady has not, however, rendered him frail or needy. He has remained fiercely independent and strong throughout his first and second bouts with this lung cancer, taking early retirement from his university professorship, meeting the situation head on, remaining pro-active in his treatment, and continuing to enjoy life.

On the fifteen-minute drive to his apartment, we speculate as to why Ed has called us and how the day may unfold. He greets us warmly when we arrive and gets right to the point. "I'm having trouble swallowing," he says simply. " I'd like you to take me to the hospital so we can find out what's happening." He writes me a check for some typing I've recently completed for him, picks up a small suitcase he has packed, and without further delay, he walks out of his apartment for the last time.

The drive to the hospital is a pregnant silence. Finally my husband makes a feeble attempt to give voice to his thoughts—that his father may never come out of the hospital, may never again travel these familiar streets, may never enjoy these particular sights and sounds and smells again—and asks his father how this is for him. "It's not really relevant," Ed replies.

Ed is checked into the hospital and taken for a new x-ray. When he returns, we meet his oncologist once more. The physician who makes his living working with the dying seems unable to approach the word itself or to include his own presence in our interaction. After explaining that the x-ray shows a tumor encroaching on Ed's esophagus, he gives him a gentle punch in the shoulder with his fist and in a voice raised a decibel above normal, without making eye contact with any one of us, exclaims, "Well, onward and upward! I'll check in with you later." As he walks out of the room, I am astonished that he can say nothing more authentic or warm to a patient he has known for two years and is unlikely to see again.

My husband and I sit beside the hospital bed. Time seems to stand still or race forward in little halts and spurts. There is some small talk but more silence. Words do not seem particularly appropriate or necessary. Finally Ed, who has been looking at the newspaper, insists my husband and I go out and get something to eat. I sense he wants some time alone. I watch my husband, struggling to hold back tears, bend over to kiss his father. I hear Ed say gently and matter-of-factly, "Don't worry, life goes on." I wonder if he means he believes his own life will continue in some other realm after his physical death or if he means to assure his son that life in a larger sense will go on as usual after he dies. Perhaps he intends both.

When we return to the hospital room barely an hour later, Ed's face is a different color and the energy in the room is transformed. It is unmistakably obvious that Ed has surrendered himself to the process of dying. I turn around without stopping, to find the nearest phone to call Ed's other son, who lives less than two hours away, and his brother in Philadelphia. They will both leave for the hospital as soon as possible. One will not arrive in time to say good-bye. I go back to sit with Ed while my husband telephones his mother and her husband, and also calls his father's closest companion.

When the hospital shift changes, a doctor we haven't met before introduces herself and asks us to step into the hallway with her. She says compassionately that she is sorry to meet us under the present circumstances, she doesn't expect Ed to live through the night, and that, in her view, the important thing is to keep him as comfortable as possible. She proposes giving him oxygen and morphine to make the transition easier. It is a relief to have her acknowledgment of the reality we are all facing. Since Ed has so actively orchestrated his own treatments up to this point, I feel it important to ask him if the morphine and oxygen are what he wants at this time. When I get his attention and ask, he gives me an affirmative nod and closes his eyes again, seemingly intent on the task at hand.

Ed's room fills with individuals who love him and who will stay close by until his death. There is an extra bed in the room where some people sleep from time to time. The hours pass. Shortly after midnight, Ed stirs and opens his eyes once, galvanizing the attention of everyone in the room. He glances around at the faces intent upon his. My husband and I experience the same reaction to this moment, and note his look of surprise which seems to say, "Why am I still here?" before his eyes close for the last time. Eventually the only sound inside an eerie silence saturating the room is the breath moving in and out of a dying man's body, until it slowly stops. I witness my father-in-law exit his body, gracefully, peacefully, without fear or struggle, bestowing on his children a legacy far more significant than his material possessions. I sense no end to anything, I notice that he is still contactable, that our relationship continues. This experience affects me profoundly and irrevocably alters my fear of death.

After the series of injections to boost my white count, I ask my husband to help me plan a Celebration of Life party to coincide with my birthday the following month. We send invitations, not to everyone we know, but to those individuals and families who have truly helped and supported us, in an ongoing way, during the past six months. I request yellow flowers and balloons, the color of the sun, which I feel filling my soul after a long, dark night. My husband orders two cakes. One is decorated with balloon hearts and says, "Thank you friends!" The other has a big yellow sun face, wearing sunglasses, and says, "Dawn is back!"

I obtain my daughter's permission to go without a wig for this event. All of these people have seen me without hair and I do not want to pretend that things are other than they actually are. Although I know other treatments will continue and that we cannot know what the future will hold, the relief I feel at completing the prescribed chemotherapy treatments is enormous. I have faced the lion. I have scaled the mountain "with a little help from my friends" as the song says. I think of creating a shirt for myself emblazoned with the words "I survived chemotherapy," or simply, "Happy to Be Alive!"

I petition my "weekly reader" friend who is known for devising unique rituals for special occasions to create some sort of ceremony for us to participate in during the celebration. A few key people are unable to attend, but most of the invited guests come to the gathering. The guests have been asked to bring a piece of ribbon in a kind and color that reminded them of their relationship with me in some way. Kathryn requests that I gather together some pictures of myself at various stages of my life and in various roles. She arranges the pictures between spokes of flowers reaching out to form a circle on the floor of our living room. She lights the white votive candle in my favorite lotus shaped glass container and places it in the center of the circle. She passes around some drums.

The organic, visceral experience of drumming together unites us inside the sound of a group heartbeat outside of time or space. Then, each person present is invited to comment on the ribbon he or she has chosen in relationship to me. The ribbons are tied together to form a bright and colorful friendship chain. My resolve to let love in, to let love heal, is strengthened as I meet the challenge of staying present and open to the energy and to the beams of light streaming toward me.

I become so nearly overwhelmed that when I finally have a chance to say something, I am unable to give the eloquent speech I want to give. I want to tell these special souls that their uncommon generosity, sensitivity, and kindness have saved my life. I want to thank them for valuing my life and for loving me. I want to say, "You people are my true friends. Do you recognize your extraordinary beauty? Let us dance and sing and give thanks and celebrate our aliveness!" Instead, my mouth goes dry, my tongue thickens, and it is all I can do to try once more to thank those in the room, however inadequately, for their assistance and support in the weeks and months and minutes that have brought us to this moment of sharing.

"You can sleep but you can't hide," my father says to me in a visit we have during a dream. He also says I will live a long time and that I will not die of cancer.

My husband takes our daughter on their annual summer trip together and I have a week alone in the house. The normalcy of their going is a relief. While they are away, a group of Tibetan monks arrives at a spiritual center near our home. The theme of their week-long visit is healing. They will create a sand mandala, gives talks on Tibetan healing practices, and offer healing sessions to groups and individuals. I add my name to a waiting list.

Photographer: Barry Barankin

Sand mandala nearing completion

The monks, draped in their traditional burgundy and orange colored cotton robes, work on the mandala in shifts, four at a time, for many hours a day. They work mindfully, skillfully, serenely in a silence broken only by the scrapping sounds of the wooden sticks rubbing against the brass tubes of colored sand. It is the vibration that releases the sand from the tubes as they are held at just the right angle and in just the right place over the table. A tape of Tibetan chants sometimes plays in the background, the sounds sanctifying the space containing the monks, the emerging mandala, and those observing or meditating.

I return daily to re-enter the space and to marvel at the monks' impeccable focus, concentration, and precision in creating such a perfect vision of exquisite beauty. The mandala will be dismantled after its completion in five days. The sand will be scattered, given back to the sea and the image will cease to exist except in the memories of those who looked upon it. It is a powerful and dramatic symbol, a reminder that all things change, all things perish, and that impermanence is a condition of life.

There is an innate sweetness and joy in the countenance of the monks that is infectious, disarming, and refreshing. When the monks speak, their eyes smile. When they chant, the sonorous sounds are unimaginable, unrepeatable. These sounds seem to come from somewhere deep in the center of the earth, yet they emerge from the bodies of men and flow outward through their mouths. The tones and overtones are deeply melodious and vibratory and they resonate inside my soul.

The healing session is restful, restorative. There are five bald people in the room… four Tibetan monks and me (though before we leave, the woman next to me confesses that she's never had the courage to go without her wig and says she thinks my bald head is beautiful). I ask for prayers for the return of my physical strength and for help in staying conscious in regard to healing and maintaining a healthy body.

In the middle of the meditation for healing, the words "do what you love, the money will come" suddenly jump into my mind. The phrase presents itself in bold, white letters as if sprawled across a chalkboard. I try to put it aside, to concentrate on what the monk is saying and on the reverberating sounds of the glorious bell he is ringing above my head, but the words keep reforming and repeating themselves. I finally take in the thought, let it become part of my healing, let go of my image of what might occur during this time. I invite the Medicine Buddha, the healing Buddha, to reside within me. I let go of all suffering and negativity. I ask to be released from cancer. I ask that my family may be released from their suffering and for all beings to be released from suffering. I emerge from the ninety-minute session feeling strengthened, empowered, lightened.

My very new hair is like duck down, so soft that everyone wants to keep touching it. It seems to be much darker than my old hair was.

I've neither read nor heard any explanation for this color change but am told it is common. Walking through the halls of Mercy Care Center today, two different staff workers address me as "Sister," presumably because of my nearly bald head. I take their mistake as a great compliment.

A friend calls to tell me of a healer coming to our area. She says this woman has a very credible reputation and urges me to go see her. She says the healer does not charge for her sessions but accepts

A few days after last chemotherapy infusion!

donations. I am open to support for my continued healing in all venues and forms. I make an appointment to see her.

Mama Lucas has dark black skin covering a huge body and an even larger spirit. She reminds me a bit of Ammachi, an East Indian teacher who comes to California once a year, whose love could fill an ocean. Like her, Mama Lucas is conscious of her relationship to the divine and of her ability to let God work through her. She touches me with compassionate and knowing hands, full of warmth and love. She prays for many minutes, asking God over and over to send any cancer cells, which may be lingering in my body, to the "river of forgetfulness." I feel certain God is listening.

I am experiencing symptoms similar to the ones I had before my cancer diagnosis—erratic bowel movements, lots of gas and abdominal discomfort. I reason that knowing is always better than continuing to wonder. In a moment of panic or power—I'm not sure which—I call the medical center to request a blood test and a CT scan, startling my oncologist who knows my dread of needle sticks.

Although this is my fourth CT scan, it is my first time to go to the hospital unaccompanied for the procedure. I walk upstairs to the infusion unit to get a needle put in my arm for the CT scan. Bella has me sit down in one of the recliners and puts the electric heating pad over my arm to warm it. A woman directly across from me in the same kind of chair is holding her husband's hand and asking the nurses all kinds of questions. Bella and Cherie keep referring to me as a survivor, remarking on how much hair I have now and how well I look.

Cherie brings out a glass bottle, which I recognize as containing one of the chemotherapy drugs I received. Addressing the woman she says cheerily, "This is the juice." The cancer patient responds by asking, "Will I feel it going in?" Realizing she is about to experience chemotherapy for the first time, I yearn to say something comforting, reassuring, yet I'm not sure what might actually be helpful or accurate. Her anxiety floats across the space between us as we observe one another in a weighty silence. Finally her husband asks if my hair came back in a different color. After talking longer than necessary about my new hair, I ask his wife if she is here for the first time. She nods yes and manages a weak smile. Thinking how much it helped me to be told so, I finally venture, "Just remember that each time is different and no matter how you feel, it won't necessarily be the same each time you get an infusion." Suddenly doubting my communication will be at all helpful, I want to be anywhere else but where I am and my mind exits the room before my body.

To my surprise, no one else is waiting when I reach the end of the long yellow line marking the way to the scanning room. The technician is one I haven't seen before. He has just the right mix of humor, kindness, and aptitude which has the effect of putting me almost immediately at ease. His touch is gentle and reassuring as he helps me onto the table and gently places my arms in the familiar position above my head. He asks if I have been through chemotherapy and mentions that his wife received chemotherapy for breast cancer. I have come prepared this time—extra water in the car to drink after the procedure, tampon in, no metal on my clothing. I am prepared for the metallic taste in my mouth, the tingling in my arm as the dye enters my body, the warmth in my pelvis that will make me think I need to urinate.

For some inexplicable reason, none of these reactions occur to a significant degree this time. The scan itself seems to go more quickly than on previous visits. It feels as if the technician is working with me instead of on me. I am out of the hospital in less than one hour.

Feeling almost euphoric, I go shopping for gifts needed for upcoming events. At home an hour later I am suddenly exhausted. When I try to work I cannot concentrate. Every time I start to read I feel like going to sleep. Finally I realize that the fifteen minutes spent in the infusion room was emotionally re-stimulating. It has triggered physical and mental responses in me that I had not anticipated.

A friend tells me she can't even walk past the hospital where she received her chemotherapy treatments without feeling nauseous. Another friend shares that she still experiences abject anxiety before her yearly mammogram even though she has been cancer-free for fifteen years.

Sometimes it seems almost impossible to control the doubts and fears that arise in my mind. In a casual conversation with the parent of one of my daughter's friends, who turns out to be an oncologist, I mention the type of my ovarian cancer and she replies, "Oh, we don't like clear cell!" She hastens to add that Taxol is an effective drug and that "it can be used again." My mind attaches itself to her words and takes on the implied assumption that the cancer probably will come back, and then leaps into a fantasy of recurrent cancer, recurrent treatment, and eventual death. It takes a great deal of energy to bridle these thoughts and re-structure my thinking.

I feel relieved and understood when my surgeon oncologist says that for the cancer patient, the time after completion of treatment can sometimes be more challenging than the treatment itself. During treatment one feels he or she is doing something active to reclaim a healthy body. After treatment is over, a waiting game begins. Paranoia is common. Feelings can vacillate. It is an adjustment period. Each person must find his or her own way.

My other oncologist tells me to pick one day a month and let all my fears and anxieties about a cancer recurrence surface on that day but not to let it take over my mind the rest of the month. I think he is suggesting that I try to regain some perspective and refuse to let my fears and fantasies about what could happen run or ruin my life.

When I go in for my monthly acupuncture treatment, Isaac says that there has not been nearly enough time for a new cancer to grow to the point where I would be able to feel it. He reminds me that there are many other causes of all my symptoms. When my CA-125 test is still extremely low and my CT scan clear, I eventually figure out that the stomach cramps, bloating, and gas are a reaction to a particular soy product, overly consumed. This is something I have complete control over.

Are there people who simply jump back into life after a cancer diagnosis and treatment, who go on as if nothing has happened? Is it possible that such people never look back or give the cancer another thought? If so, I don't think I will be one of those people. I fear I will be more like the man who said that after cancer you always have that bit of fear, that it never goes away, and every little physical symptom you have, you think it's the cancer coming back.

Will it get easier if I make it through the designated two to three year period when my cancer is most likely to come back? I think of a woman whose cancer returned after eight years and another who experienced a recurrence at twelve years and again at sixteen years after treatment. I remember the woman who got an entirely different kind of cancer a decade later. I remember a friend who, a year after completing chemotherapy for breast cancer, beamed when she said she was so happy to just have a common cold. Will my first thought always be that it's the cancer come back no matter what or how minor the health problem may be? Will I ever still the nagging little voice that says no matter what I do, no matter how vigilant I am, the cancer could return at any time? It feels like a burden, until one day I realize that perhaps it is a boon.

In his thought-provoking book, *From Age-ing to Sage-ing,* Rabbi Zalman Schacter-Shalomi talks about a hospice counselor who developed colon cancer when she was 67 years old. Her illness made her realize how often she said yes when she needed to say no. Her deep encounter with death liberated her from this form of self-betrayal. Years later, she stated that her encounter with death initiated her into "states of inner freedom I could scarcely imagine when I was younger."[9] She goes on to say that though her cancer had not returned in years, she never wants it to leave entirely. "I want it to sit on my left shoulder for the remainder of my life because the encounter with death gives me the authority to claim my own voice and sing my own song."[10]

Now comes the really hard work—a task that seems almost more formidable than chemotherapy—the challenge of re-creating my life in a way that will sustain my newfound consciousness, of finding a way to live that promotes my continued health and well-being, and that promotes balance and harmony in my life on an ongoing basis.

Our often fast-paced and stress-filled lives can wear us down physically and emotionally. I have an article in my files giving the results of a survey indicating that 70% of Americans feel they work more hours than they would like to work, and that 65% feel stressed by this situation. Another article quotes a billboard emblazoned with the message "You Can Rest When You're Dead" and points out that in our society, we are often in such a hurry to succeed, to pack each moment with adventure, that we don't leave ourselves any time to enjoy, to reflect, to rejoice, to be grateful, to rest. The author of this article, Naomi Levy, notes that rest was once viewed as a divine activity and as a sign of holiness and wisdom, rather than as a symbol of laziness or weakness.

I can remember a time in my childhood when stores were not open on Sundays, or even on Saturday nights. Days of rest, in various religious traditions, were actually observed, spent in worship, in nature, or in quiet time with family. I wonder how our lives as a culture might change, if for one day each week or even part of each day, we unplugged the telephones, televisions, and computers, turned off our car engines and spent quality time resting, reflecting, walking, meditating in silence, or being in conscious contact and communion with others?

My experience is that when we do observe such practices, everything changes. Our souls are replenished, we treat others better, our lives take on a richer texture and a more authentic quality. For those of us raising families and furthering careers in urban American society, making rest and reflection a routine part of life requires attention, commitment, and vigilance. It is not always easy and distractions abound, yet surely this is a worthwhile project.

Sometimes I worry that without the active needle prick of cancer to keep reminding me I may lose my newly found attentiveness to life; I may fall off the keen edge of awareness I now carry through my days. What if my present clear focus hazes over? What if I stay well but fall into inertia and begin taking life for granted? I don't want the cancer to come back because I haven't fully gotten the lesson. Nor do I want to worry the cancer back into existence!

I resolve never again to let myself become as stressed as I was before my cancer diagnosis. I resolve to continue listening to my body and to give it what it needs when it is begging for attention. I resolve to live my life as a spiritual practice, to live a healthy life, a balanced life, a conscious life. I remind myself of Rabbi Groesberg's words whispered in my ear after my cancer diagnosis, "Remember, anything is possible," and I think to myself... yes, even this is possible. I can stay awake! I can pay attention! I can achieve balance in my life.

A year after completing chemotherapy, as I continue to take herbs three times daily and receive acupuncture once a month to deal with lingering aftereffects such as peripheral neuropathy, and to continue strengthening my immune system, I feel strong enough to give a residential meditation retreat known as a two-week Enlightenment Intensive. Although I have led many three-day Enlightenment Intensives, I wish to claim this deeper challenge and experience.

In addition to attracting participants and making sure the environment supports the purpose of the Intensive, I know that this endeavor will require setting aside my own agenda and letting go of personal concerns in order to be fully present for others. It will require keeping my attention on the individuals in the group instead of on the chatter of their minds. It will require maintaining a steady course, supporting the participants in facing whatever barriers may arise, and in getting through whatever crises may occur during the course of the Intensive. It will require making myself available to the participants and the staff every day (and even in the middle of the night if the situation arises).

Friends who have given this type of Intensive warn me about how fatiguing and grueling it will be for me; some are concerned that it may be too taxing on my body. I feel certainty about leading the Intensive. I am committed to making it happen. I am excited about providing such an opportunity for those who yearn for a deeper experience of Truth in their lives. I enlist Willow to come and cook for the event, making the menu primarily macrobiotic.

At the end of the two weeks someone asks, "Was it hard?" My first response is, "Hard compared to what? Having cancer? Going through six months of chemotherapy? Parenting a teenager?" The two-week retreat was much like life in a magnified form. There were periods of confusion, periods of clarity, periods of chaos, periods of peace. There were moments of despair, panic, and sorrow and moments of hope, bliss, and joy. There was drama, ecstasy, emotionality, conflict, change, and genuine shifts in consciousness. Crises arose and were handled. Nobody left or died. We all made it through and went on with our journeys, albeit with heightened awareness and sensitivity, profound new insights, and in some cases, fundamentally changed.

We meet a woman during our family's annual sojourn at family camp who shares a remarkable story. Nearly thirty years ago, her husband, in seemingly perfect health after a physical check-up two weeks before, died quite suddenly of a heart attack at age 54. Two weeks later this woman, somewhat younger than her husband, was diagnosed with renal cancer. She had a kidney removed and got a job in order to continue raising her four children. Some years later, her cancer came back. Chemotherapy did not seem to help and she had one lung removed. At the time we meet this attractive lady, now in her seventies and looking very fit, her cancer has manifest once again. She has recently had a large tumor in her neck removed though doctors were not able to "get it all." She says she is treating her cancer through diet, exercise, and meditation. She works in the Resource Library at a large medical center. The day my husband and a friend of ours climb to the top of Sentinel Dome in Yosemite National Park, she is already there enjoying the view.

A Buddhist minister, teacher, and friend of ours, is fond of saying that life is a bumpy road. The picture he often draws to accompany his words is actually a horizontal wavy line reminding one of hills and valleys or the surge of the sea. In other words, the road of life is not often straight, paved, and smooth. It is more frequently a series of ups and downs, not to mention a few mean potholes! Sometimes the scenery is so mesmerizing we hardly notice the bumps; sometimes we can navigate around them; and, as Ken Kesey once said, "Sometimes there is no way out but through." A sudden, unexpected dip in the road can be quite a shock and can even result in some nasty bruises, yet that dip may be just the wake-up call that is needed. Eventually we may come to realize that the smooth spaces are not necessarily better or to be preferred over the rough ones—it's just the way the road is.

I try to get across to those whom I train to work with the elderly and the ill through COMPASSIONATE TOUCH® that if they are truly present during their sessions, with their full and unconditional attention on the individual, then ending the session will usually not be difficult. If the student has allowed him or herself to remain open

Photographer: James Dawson

Demonstrating Compassionate Touch® techniques during photo shoot for a magazine article

to and in contact with that individual, then that person will feel touched on some level. Whether physical contact has taken place or not, that person will feel complete, acknowledged, and accepted. The relationship will have been fulfilling.

I suspect that if we allow ourselves to be fully present and engaged in life, accepting whatever occurs as part of life, then when it is time to say good-bye to our physical existence, it will not be so difficult. If we continually shrink or hide from life, try to make it be different, deny its actuality, accept only the parts that look or feel good to us, or if we stand outside of life and watch it as if it were a video tape, then we will always feel unfulfilled and no matter how long we have been given to live, it will be difficult to say good-bye.

Birth inevitably leads to death. Life is full of uncertainty, brief at best, and its length is unpredictable. We cannot know what will happen next week or even in the next moment. It is accepting the reality of impermanence that reveals to us the preciousness of each moment.

I do not know if I will die of cancer, from some other disease, from some catastrophic natural disaster, from getting hit by a truck, or from my heart giving out at a very old age. I may die at any moment on any day of any number of things, just like everyone else in the world. When I do die, I am nearly certain, life itself will go on.

In Hawaii, 13 months after cancer diagnosis

Conclusion

What saves us is to take a step. Then another step.
It's always the same step but it must be taken.

Antoine De Saint-Exupery

You make friends with cancer by accepting it for what it is, by heeding its call to consciousness, by letting it change your life. You slow down. You pay attention. You stop doing things you don't really want or need to do. You prioritize. You cultivate patience. You pace yourself. You listen to your body, and you respect it. You spend time with those who love you for who and what you are and with those whose presence is healing.

You make friends with cancer by noticing the myriad miracles life offers daily—the chorus of bird songs in the morning air, the intoxicating fragrance of one pink rose, the melody of raindrops, the heart-melting sweetness of your children's smiles, the eternality of an ocean wave, the exquisite beauty of a setting sun, the presence of your beloved—which, before cancer, you may have overlooked or been too "busy" to enjoy or appreciate.

You make friends with cancer by letting love in. You open your heart. You tell the truth. You ask for help. You accept the profound generosity of friends. You let whatever you may have given return itself to you.

You make friends with cancer by allowing it to remind you of what is actually important in life and what is less so, by forging a relationship with it that fosters new insight. You push through the limits of your conscious awareness until you begin to see the uninvited guest not as an adversary, but as an unexpected opportunity for learning and growth.

You make friends with cancer by expanding your vision, by welcoming the gift of each new dawn, by breathing in the myriad colors, sounds, and scents of beauty in the space outside your window. You don't waste time complaining about that which you cannot change or about what you wish were different. You notice what you have instead of what you don't have. You laugh and sing and dance when you can; you weep when you must. You come out of hiding. You participate in life as fully as you are able. You realize that happiness is a state of mind, attainable in any circumstance. You practice gratitude and forgiveness.

With Barry, Meghan and Whitney one year after last chemotherapy

You make friends with cancer not by hating it or fighting with it but by acknowledging its presence, accepting what it has to teach you. You take the first step in the rest of your Journey. Sometimes you inch forward, sometimes you lurch, sometimes you pause to rest, sometimes you march, and sometimes you leap, but mostly you just keep going, one step at a time.

Annotated Bibliography

The following list is by no means a complete one of available books on the subject of coping with cancer. These books are simply the ones that I found most useful in my personal experience with cancer and cancer treatment, or books that I have used in working with cancer patients and their families.

Adams, Patch, M.D. with Maureen Mylander, <u>Gesundheit: Bringing Good Health to You, the Medical System, and Society through Physician Service, Complementary Therapies, Humor and Joy,</u> Healing Arts Press, Rochester, Vermont, 1993.

> This book reveals the unique vision of Patch Adams, activist, visionary, social revolutionary, clown, and healer, and chronicles his quest to transform our health care system.

Albom, Mitch, Tuesdays with Morrie: <u>An old man, a young man, and life's greatest lesson,</u> Doubleday, New York, 1997.

> In this wise and wonderful book, the author shares the courage, insight and wisdom of Morrie Schwartz, his favorite college professor, who, years later, is facing death from ALS. Albom passes on the gift of his last tutorial from this great teacher in this unique and moving book which has much to teach us all.

Babcock, Elise NeeDell, <u>When Life Becomes Precious: A Guide for Loved Ones and Friends of Cancer Patients,</u> Bantam Books, New York, 1997.

> An invaluable resource, with hundreds of practical and applicable tips for friends, family members, and caregivers of those experiencing cancer or any other serious illness. One of the best chapters includes a list "52 Gifts You Can Give" to offer support to those living with cancer.

Bolen, Jean Shinoda, <u>Close to the Bone: Life-threatening Illness and the Search for Meaning,</u> Touchstone, New York, 1998.

> Dr. Bolen's rich understanding of the human condition in both archetypal and individual form, inhabits all her books. In this book she details the value of illness, loss and death, viewed as a soul journey, or spiritual initiation, drawing from the experiences of clients and friends as well as from her own.

Breathnach, Sarah Ban, <u>Simple Abundance: A Daybook of Comfort and Joy,</u> Warner Books, New York, 1995.

> I would call this a "woman's book." I almost never fail to find some lesson, some practical advice, some prescient reminder when I open it, no matter which of the 366 days' essays I choose to read. The few that seem superficial I simply skip over.

Canfield, Jack, Mark Victor Hansen, Patty Aubery, and Nancy Mitchell, <u>Chicken Soup for the Surviving Soul,</u> Health Communications Inc., Deerfield Beach, Florida, 1996.

> This book contains poems, stories, and shared experiences of individuals and close friends or family members of individuals who have lived with cancer and survived cancer treatment. Some of these people are famous, some not, some still alive, some not. It made me laugh and cry and it soothed by soul.

Chödrön, Pema, <u>When Things Fall Apart: Heart Advice for Difficult Times,</u> Shambala, Boston, Massachusetts, 1997.

> I was introduced to Pema Chödrön, an American Buddhist nun and the director of Gampo Abbey in Nova Scotia, during my recovery from cancer surgery when a friend brought me a series of cassette tapes of her talks. My mind and my spirit resonate deeply with what she has to say.

_____, <u>The Wisdom of No Escape and the Path of Loving-Kindness,</u> Shambala, Boston, Massachusetts, 1991.

> This book helped me put my cancer diagnosis into perspective and continues to nourish my soul. I read from it frequently for centering, for guidance, for inspiration, and to partake of Pema's wisdom.

Clifford, Christine and Jack Lindstrom (illustrator), <u>Not Now... I'm Having a No Hair Day: Humor and Healing for People with Cancer</u>, Pfeifer-Hamilton Publishers, 1996.

Laughter is thought to boost the immune system. Besides, we all need to lighten up sometimes and take our woes less seriously! This is a light, little book that might help. A few of the cartoons, many about hair loss and baldness, actually made me laugh out loud.

Cotter, Arlene, From This Moment On: A Guide for Those Recently Diagnosed with Cancer, Random House, New York, 1999.

Written in an easy-to-read, unique style, this recently published book is worth its rather high price ($25.00 paperback). I read it from cover to cover and immediately loaned it to an acquaintance newly diagnosed with breast cancer.

Diamond, W. John, M.D., and W. Lee Cowden, M.D. with Burton Goldberg, An Alternative Medicine Definitive Guide to Cancer, Future Medicine Publishing, Inc., Tiburon, California, 1997.

Aside from being a great doorstop and paperweight, this book is a comprehensive educational tool. Twenty-three physicians contribute to the section on successful cancer treatment plans using multiple therapies and remedies. Another section contains a guide to innovative approaches, anti-cancer substances and support therapies for reversing cancer, and a third section deals with the politics, detection, and prevention of cancer.

Dobic, Milenka 'Mina', My Beautiful Life: How Macrobiotics Brought Me from Cancer to Radiant Life, Findhorn Press, Inc., Tallahassee, Florida, 2000.

The author of this just-published book was diagnosed with Stage IV (metastasized) ovarian cancer and given two months to live in 1987. A doctor friend gave her two books: Recalled by Life and The Cancer Prevention Diet. She read them and made a dramatic decision that saved her life. The difference in this book and other personal story books about women with ovarian cancer is that the author is cancer-free and alive today. Tracing her journey from Yugoslavia to Massachusetts to California, from sickness to health, and from patient to healer/teacher, her book is insightful, instructive, and inspiring.

Drum, David, Making the Chemotherapy Decision, Lowell House, 1996.

I wish I had read this book before I got cancer or while I was going through chemotherapy treatment. Though I do not necessarily agree with everything it says, it contains a great deal of useful information, good advice, and pragmatic suggestions

about how to tolerate chemotherapy treatment and how to cope
with its side effects.

Falk, Marcia, <u>The Book of Blessings: New Jewish Prayers for Daily Life, The
Sabbath, and the New Moon Festival</u>, Beacon Press, Boston, 1996.

> A Hebrew scholar, translator, poet, and spiritual feminist, Marcia
> Falk offers vital, gender free translations of traditional readings
> and fresh, new, poetic images which go straight to the heart of
> the matter and to the heart of the reader.

Hansel, Tim, <u>You Gotta Keep Dancin': In the Midst of Life's Hurts, You Can
Choose Joy!</u> Chariot Victor Publishing, Colorado Springs, Colorado, 1985.

> The title of this book reached out and grabbed me as I was
> walking through a drugstore recently. Written from the author's
> personal Christian perspective and uplifting for anyone who has
> suffered traumatic physical loss, for anyone living with chronic
> pain or just as inspirational reading.

Harpham, Wendy Schlessel, M.D., <u>After Cancer: A Guide to Your New Life</u>,
HarperCollins, New York, 1994.

> Written in question and answer format, this book covers bases
> that others don't. The author provides important information for
> cancer survivors as well as for their friends and families. The nine
> Appendices are as helpful as the chapters.

_____, <u>When a Parent Has Cancer: A Guide to Caring for Your
Children</u>, HarperCollins, New York, 1997.

> When I found out I had cancer, I hoped that a book like this one
> existed and a friend finally found it for me. Mother of three, a
> physician and cancer survivor, the author writes with authority,
> honesty, and clarity that can come only from direct experience.
> Full of useful and pragmatic advice for parents with children of
> all ages, the book is also encouraging and comforting. Included
> as an insert is an excellent little book, <u>Becky and the Worry Cup</u>,
> for children to read alone or together with a parent.

Harwell, Amy with Kristine Tomasik, <u>When Your Friend Gets Cancer: How
you can help</u>, Harold Shaw Publishers, Wheaton, Illinois, 1987.

> An easy to read and practical book that offers sensible and
> compassionate guidance on how to be a friend when someone
> you love has cancer.

Kramp, Erin Tierney and Douglas H. Kramp, with Emily McKhann, <u>Living with the End in Mind: A Practical Checklist for Living Life to the Fullest by Embracing Your Mortality</u>, Three Rivers Press, New York, 1998.

> This unique and heartfelt book offers a life-affirming process for preparing for death. It presents a thoughtful, practical approach for dealing with the issues of mortality whether one has been diagnosed with a terminal illness or is in perfect health.

Kushi, Michio, <u>The Macrobiotic Way: The Complete Macrobiotic Diet and Exercise Book</u>, Avery Publishing Group, Inc., New Jersey, 1985.

> The classic Macrobiotic primer and comprehensive guide for those interested in the philosophy, principles, and application of macrobiotics as a healing diet or as a life-style.

_____, <u>The Cancer Prevention Diet: Michio Kushi's Nutritional Blueprint for the Prevention and Relief of Disease</u>, St. Martin's Griffin, New York, 1993.

> Updated since the original appeared in 1983, this book is well-researched and full of medical evidence not generally known. It is one of the best books I know that details the link between diet and cancer. It gives specific information and recommendations for healing from different kinds of cancer and contains a wealth of useful material but needs to be digested in stages and well before one faces a life-threatening disease such as cancer.

LeShan, Lawrence, <u>Cancer as a Turning Point: A Handbook for People with Cancer, Their Families, and Health Professionals</u>, the Penguin Group, New York, 1990.

> Summarizing a lifetime of work as a psychotherapist working with cancer patients, this book is full of stories, insights, and wisdom based on LeShan's clinical experience and research.

LeVert, Suzanne, <u>When Someone You Love Has Cancer: What you must know, what you can do, what you should expect</u>, Dell Publishing, New York, 1995.

> Informative, concise, straightforward, and practical, I often recommend this book to people who wonder what to do or how they can help when a family member or a friend receives a cancer diagnosis.

Levine, Stephen, <u>A Year to Live: How to Live this Year as If It Were Your Last</u>, Crown Publishers, Inc., New York, 1997.

> Although this book might have deeper authenticity if the author actually had been given a year to live, it includes a number of life review strategies and mindfulness meditations to help decrease the reader's fear of death and increase his or her joy in living each moment. Written from a Buddhist perspective and in Stephen's usual intimate style.

_____, <u>Who Dies? An Investigation of Conscious Living and Conscious Dying</u>, Anchor Books, New York, 1982.

> Fortunately, I had read this book several times long before my own cancer diagnosis. It is just what the subtitle says it is. I recommend it as one of the truest and most important spiritual books anyone could ever read.

MacDonald, Gayle, <u>Medicine Hands: Massage Therapy for People with Cancer</u>, Findhorn Press, Inc., Tallahassee, Florida, 1999.

> When my father-in-law was dying of cancer and asked me to come to his apartment and give him a foot massage, I was happy to comply. The next day he told me his doctor said he shouldn't get any more massages because it might spread the cancer. Had this long-needed guidebook, which is beautifully written, researched and crafted, been available then, I'd have marched right into the oncologist's office and plunked it on his desk!

Northrup, Christiane, M.D., <u>Women's Bodies, Women's Wisdom: Creating Physical and Emotional Health and Healing</u>, Bantam Books, New York, 1998.

> As Caroline Myss states, this book is "A masterpiece for every woman who has an interest in her body, her mind, and her soul." The author has a unique feminist physician's approach. It is a comprehensive look at women and health, offering information on a broad range of topics and answering many questions.

Ornish, Dean, M.D. <u>Love and Survival: The Scientific Basis for the Healing Power of Intimacy</u>, HarperCollins, New York, 1998.

> Some new friends left this book, with a loving inscription, on my doorstep along with a vase of flowers while I was undergoing chemotherapy. I have experienced its premise—that love is ultimately the most powerful healing agent that we can access—to be true. It is an insightful book, which has much to teach us in regard to health, healing, and quality of life.

Remen, Rachel Naomi, M.D. Kitchen Table Wisdom: Stories That Heal, Riverhead Books, New York, 1996.

Two different people sent me this book soon after I was diagnosed with cancer. It is authentic, personal, powerful, inspirational. I would recommend it to everyone who likes to read and who is interested in healing on any level.

Remoff, Heather Trexler, February Light: A Love Letter to the Seasons During a Year of Cancer, St. Martins Press, New York, 1997.

A personal story of one woman's recovery from ovarian cancer— part medical diary, part nature journal, and part personal reflection. It is skillfully written and easy to read. The author's attitude of "beating this bastard cancer" seems to work well for her.

Ryan, M. J., editor, A Grateful Heart: Daily blessings for the Evening Meal from Buddha to the Beatles, Conari Press, Berkeley, California, 1994.

We keep this book on our kitchen table and take turns reading from it before family meals.

Ryder, Brent G., Editor, The Alpha Book on Cancer and Living: For Patients, Family and Friends, The Alpha Institute, 1993.

This book offers a wide range of information on everything from treatment options to legal and financial concerns for cancer survivors. Thorough, well documented, attractively laid out and easy to access, this book is an invaluable information resource, which also offers a great deal of practical guide for cancer patients, families, friends, caregivers.

Schachter-Shalomi, Zalman and Ronald S. Miller, From Age-ing to Sage-ing: A Profound New Vision of Growing Older, Warner Books, New York, 1995.

When I met Rabbi Schachter-Shalomi, I was struck with his buoyant spirit, his zest for living, and the twinkle in his eyes. When I heard him speak, I was impressed with his story telling ability, his compassionate heart and his unique vision. I bought tapes of his talks and I bought his book so I could have ongoing access to his unique brand of wisdom. I recommend this book to anyone interested in aging gracefully and in making peace with his or her mortality.

Schimmel, Selma R. with Barry Fox, Cancer Talk: Voices of Hope and Endurance from "The Group Room," the World's Largest Cancer Support Group, Broadway Books, New York, 1999.

> A unique book consisting of transcripts from a call-in radio talk show which had as one of its goals helping those with cancer feel empowered rather than victimized by their disease. Contains useful insights and stories on a wide range of subjects, from both patient and physician perspectives. At the end of the book is a list of 100 cancer support and advocacy organizations, including web site addresses.

Schwartz, Morrie, Letting Go, Dell Publishing, New York, 1996.

> This book offers, from his own mouth, words and stories of Morrie Schwartz whose life and death have been so movingly chronicled in the book and television movie, Tuesdays with Morrie. The book is candid, pithy, inspirational.

Siegel, Bernie S., M.D. Peace, Love and Healing: Bodymind Communication and the Path to Self-Healing: An Exploration, Harper and Row, New York, 1989.

> A thought-provoking book which reflects on new ways of thinking about health and healing and the mind/body connection. The book is a synthesis of what the author has learned since he wrote Love, Medicine and Miracles with a continued emphasis on creativity and self-healing.

Tilberis, Liz, No Time to Die: Living with Ovarian Cancer, Avon Books, Inc., New York, 1998.

> Probably best known as editor-in-chief of Harper's Bazaar magazine and for her connections to famous people such as Princess Diana, this book documents Liz Tilberis's personal odyssey with Stage III ovarian cancer. Though she lost her very active battle with recurring cancer shortly after her book was published, hers is a passionate and fascinating memoir.

Turner, Kristina, The Self-Healing Cookbook: A Macrobiotic Primer for Healing Body, Mind and Moods with Whole, Natural Foods, Earthtones Press, l996.

> This is my favorite cookbook because it contains so much more than good recipes. It integrates humor, compassion, psychology, and spirituality with valuable information on nutrition and

macrobiotic cooking. It is easy to read, down to earth, and immensely useful for anyone who wants to eat a healthier diet in a more conscious way.

Walters, Richard, Options: The Alternative Cancer Therapy Book, Avery Publishing Group, New York, 1993.

This book contains a full spectrum of information on alternative treatments from herbal, nutritional, and holistic approaches to metabolic medicine, although nothing of Native American healing practices is mentioned. Written in layman's language the book is an excellent synopsis of research and a good starting place for those who want to make informed decisions in choosing alternative or adjunct cancer treatments outside the medical profession.

Weil, Andrew, M.D., Health and Healing, Houghton Mifflin Company, New York, 1995

I find all of Andrew Weil's books easy to read and helpful. Dr. Weil is able to assist readers in understanding the strengths and weaknesses of both conventional and alternative therapies in a healing process. He stresses making wise and informed choices and striving for a healthy balance.

_____, Natural Health, Natural Medicine: A Comprehensive Manual for Wellness and Self-Care, Houghton Mifflin, Boston, Massachusetts, 1990.

This book is overflowing with judicious and sensible advice for staying healthy. It is an invaluable reference manual and guidebook for health care.

Wilber, Ken, Grace and Grit: Spirituality and Healing in the Life and Death of Treya Killam Wilbur, Shambala, Boston, 1991.

Attempting to be a personal diary, a love story, a philosophical overview, and a spiritual guide all at once, this book chronicles Ken and Treya's five year journey with cancer—from the original diagnosis ten days after their marriage, to her death at age 41. It covers their experiences with both conventional and alternative treatments throughout recurrences, metastases and other health problems that occurred for each of them. Not an easy read but honest, thought provoking, and often compelling.

Winawer, Sidney J., M.D. with Nick Taylor, <u>Healing Lessons</u>, Routledge, New York, 1999.

This poignant book communicates the power of love and a traumatic event to foster new thinking and personal growth. It tells the personal story of a physician and cancer expert who is forced to look at this disease from a new perspective when his wife is diagnosed with a deadly, metastatic cancer. He supports her search for alternative and unproven therapies to supplement more conventional treatments. Her life-prolonging approach also serves to broaden the author's ideas about healing, and leads him to develop an Integrative Medicine Program at the Sloan-Kettering Cancer Center.

Appendix

Ovarian Cancers Facts

Risk Factors

Women who have not had children are at increased risk as are women with a family history of breast, ovarian, or non-polyposis colon cancer. Women who have used oral contraceptives appear to be at decreased risk. Women who are lactose intolerant and therefore cannot tolerate dairy products are at a lower risk for ovarian cancer.

Signs and Symptoms

An ovarian cancer can grow to considerable size before it causes any symptoms. This cancer is often without obvious signs or symptoms until late in its development. The first symptom may be vague discomfort in the lower abdomen, indigestion, or other mild gastrointestinal problems. Symptoms can eventually include abdominal bloating or swelling, anemia, weight loss, frequent urination, and pelvic pain.

Cause

The cause of ovarian cancer is unknown. It is most common among postmenopausal women. The risk increases with age and peaks in the eighth decade.

POSSIBLE CONTRIBUTORS

Ovarian cancer incidence is known to be highest in countries with the highest consumption of dairy foods (Sweden, Denmark, and Switzerland) and lowest in countries with low dairy intake (Japan, Hong Kong, and Singapore). Cottage cheese and yogurt appear to be the worst culprits.

NEW CASES

There were approximately 25,200 new cases of ovarian cancer in the United States in 1999 and an estimated 14,500 deaths. It now ranks second among gynecologic cancers, although more women die of ovarian cancers than of any other cancer of the reproductive system.

PREVENTION AND DETECTION

There are no known ways to prevent ovarian cancer. Regular pelvic examinations are recommended for early detection. A Pap test, used in detecting cervical cancer, rarely detects ovarian cancer. A CA-125 blood test can be a marker for ovarian cancer but is not always reliable. A normal CA-125 level does not guarantee that a woman does not have ovarian cancer.

TREATMENT

The conventional medical treatment for ovarian cancer is surgery. The extent of the surgery depends on the specific type of cancer and its stage. If the cancer has already spread beyond an ovary, then both ovaries and the uterus, as well as selected lymph nodes and surrounding structures through which the cancer typically spreads, are removed.

After surgery, typically chemotherapy and/or radiation therapies are used to destroy any remaining small areas that cannot be surgically removed and any microscopic cancer cells found in the abdominal fluids.

SURVIVAL

At least ten different types of ovarian cancer are recognized. Survival rates differ according to type. The overall relative survival rate for all stages is about 50% but varies according to differences in the aggressiveness of particular cancers and in the immune response of different women against the cancer. The survival rates for regional and distant disease are 79% and 28% respectively.

DEMOGRAPHICS

In the United States in 1999, more women died of ovarian cancer in California than in any other state (1,500) followed by Florida and New York with 1,000 deaths each and Texas with 900. Colorado, Delaware, Hawaii, Idaho, Rhode Island, South Dakota, and Wyoming reported no ovarian cancer deaths in 1999.

If you experience any of the symptoms of ovarian cancer, see a doctor immediately. Request a pelvic exam and an ultrasound or a CT scan

SOURCES

American Cancer Society Cancer Facts and Figures, 1999.

John Hopkins Symptoms and Remedies, Revised and Updated Edition, 1999.

The Merck Manual of Medical Information, Home Edition, Merck Research Laboratories, New Jersey, 1997.

Women's Bodies, Women's Wisdom: Creating Physical and Emotional Health and Healing by Dr. Christiane Northrup, 1998.

References

[1] Siegel, Dr. Bernie, <u>Love, Medicine and Miracles</u>, HarperPerennial, New York, 1990, pp.105-107.

[2] Bolen, Jean Shinoda, <u>Close to the Bone: Life-Threatening Illness and the Search for Meaning</u>, Touchstone, New York, 1998, p. 99.

[3] Ibid., p. 210.

[4] Call 1-800-850-9445 to request free copies of the "TLC" catalog.

[5] May, Herbert G. and Bruce M. Metzger, Editors, The Oxford Annotated Bible, Oxford University Press, 1962, p. 41.

[6] Ibid.

[7] Hanh, Thich Nhat, <u>Living Buddha, Living Christ</u>, Riverhead Books, New York, 1995, p. 14.

[8] Wilder, Thornton, <u>Three Plays</u>, Perennial Classics, 1995, p. 110.

[9] Schachter-Shalomi, Zalman M. and Ronald S. Miller, <u>From Age-ing to Sage-ing: A Profound New Vision of Growing Older</u>, Warner Books, New York, 1995, p. 115.

[10] Ibid.

Index

About the author

As the founder and director of COMPASSIONATE TOUCH® for those in Later Life Stages, Dawn Nelson has been a pioneer in the effort to incorporate massage and touch therapy in care plans for the frail elderly and the ill, particularly those confined to care facilities. An internationally recognized speaker, author and educator, she is also an experienced meditation teacher, communications counselor and hospice caregiver. Dawn's first book, *Compassionate Touch: Hands-On Caregiving for the Elderly, the Ill and the Dying* was recommended by one HMO medical director as "essential reading for all caregivers." Dawn lives with her husband, youngest daughter and assorted animal friends in Walnut Creek, California. She can be contacted by email: cttrain@jps.net.

About Findhorn Press

Findhorn Press is the publishing business of the Findhorn Community which has grown around the Findhorn Foundation in northern Scotland.

For a complete Findhorn Press catalogue, please contact:

Findhorn Press

The Park, Findhorn,
Forres IV36 3TY
Scotland, UK
Tel 01309 690582
freephone 0800-389 9395
Fax 01309 690036

P. O. Box 13939
Tallahassee
Florida 32317-3939, USA
Tel (850) 893 2920
toll-free 1-877-390-4425
Fax (850) 893 3442

e-mail info@findhornpress.com
findhornpress.com